W9-BGZ-989

McGRAW-HILL INDUSTRIAL ORGANIZATION
AND MANAGEMENT SERIES

L. C. MORROW, *Consulting Editor*

Practical Supervision

This book is produced in full compliance with the government's regulations for conserving paper and other essential materials.

McGRAW-HILL

INDUSTRIAL ORGANIZATION AND MANAGEMENT SERIES

L. C. MORROW, *Consulting Editor*
Editor, Factory Management and Maintenance

The program of this series has been outlined by the following advisory committee:

CHARLES WILLIAM BEESE, *Professor and Head of Department of General Engineering,* Purdue University

HAROLD V. COES, *Vice President,* Ford, Bacon & Davis

ALVIN E. DODD, *President,* The American Management Assn.

H. P. DUTTON, *Chairman, Department of Business Economics and Industrial Engineering* and *Dean, Evening Division, School of Engineering,* Illinois Institute of Technology

GLENN GARDINER, *Vice President,* Forstmann Woolen Company

JAMES W. IRWIN, *Management Counsel*

THOMAS ROY JONES, *President,* American Type Founders, Inc.

FRED A. KRAFFT, *Director of Industrial Relations,* American Viscose Corporation

HERMAN W. STEINKRAUS, *President and General Manager,* Bridgeport Brass Co.

(Books already published or in production)

BENSON—*Using Music and Sound Systems in Industry*

BETHEL, ATWATER, SMITH and STACKMAN—*Industrial Organization and Management*

BIKLEN and BRETH—*The Successful Employee Publication*

CANTOR—*Employee Counseling*

ELLS—*Salary and Wage Administration*

EVANS—*A Program for Personnel Administration*

FERN—*Training for Supervision in Industry*

FITZPATRICK—*Understanding Labor*

GARDINER—*When Foreman and Steward Bargain*

HANNAFORD—*Conference Leadership in Business and Industry*

HILL and HOOK—*Management at the Bargaining Table*

KALSEM—*Practical Supervision*

MORGAN—*Industrial Training and Testing*

PRESGRAVE—*The Dynamics of Time Study*

STOWERS—*Management Can Be Human*

WIREN and HEYEL—*Practical Management Research*

(Other titles in preparation)

Practical Supervision

BY

PALMER J. KALSEM

Engineering Educational Section
The Glenn L. Martin Company

EDITED BY

NORMAN M. JOHNSTON, Jr.

Engineering Educational Editor
The Glenn L. Martin Company

First Edition

SECOND IMPRESSION

New York *London*

MCGRAW-HILL BOOK COMPANY, INC.

1945

Practical Supervision

PRINTED IN THE UNITED STATES OF AMERICA

THE MAPLE PRESS COMPANY, YORK, PA.

To Clifford E. Roberts, Assistant Chief Engineer, The Glenn L. Martin Company, for his kindly interest and his interjection of the human-relations angle in supervisory problems

Foreword

EVERY two weeks since July 29, 1943, engineering supervisors of The Glenn L. Martin Company have received at their homes a pocket-size booklet on supervision, written to give them specific helps in their daily problems and illustrated by sprightly cartoons. Read at home, away from the worries and interruptions of the office, the booklets proved to be a painless way for supervisors to study the principles of good supervision.

Supplementing training conferences, these booklets were an integral part of a comprehensive engineering educational program. So popular were they with supervisors, that it was decided to make them available in book form. Although originally written and illustrated mainly for engineering and office supervisors, the present volume is suited for all supervisors, whether in the office, shop, or drafting room.

Retained in the book are the same qualities that made the booklets popular and meaningful: a brief, forthright style, a human-interest approach, and humorous but pointed illustrative treatment. The editorial philosophy has been to give supervisors specific knowledge of what is expected of them by their workers and management and to tell them how they can satisfy these requirements.

ROY G. ANDREWS,
Director of Engineering Personnel.

BALTIMORE, MD.,
May, 1945.

Acknowledgments

Many an engineering staff member contributed ideas to this book in informal talks with the author, who also drew upon current published literature for helpful suggestions. Members of The Glenn L. Martin Company, engineering personnel department, particularly those in the educational section, were of much assistance.

To Norman M. Johnston, Jr., goes credit for initiating the series of supervisory training bulletins which served as a basis for this book, and for using a well-directed, well-sharpened editorial blue pencil. The bulletins have been a vital part of an educational program headed by John J. Buckley, director of engineering education.

Acknowledgment is gratefully made to Roy G. Andrews, Erwin Mahannah, and Edward McFaul for reading the manuscript and making helpful suggestions, to Edwin Hall for directing the art work, to Doris Schaefer for preparing Chap. 12, to Laura Havelin for secretarial work "above and beyond the line of duty," and to Elizabeth Varnum for assisting on surveys.

Most of the cartoons are by John Gorsuch, following a style developed by Joseph Overstreet. Other illustrative work was done by Charles Wiegand and Creston Cathcart.

PALMER J. KALSEM.

BALTIMORE, MD.,
May, 1945.

Contents

1

What's Expected?

As a supervisor, what is expected of you by your workers? By management? If you can answer these questions and meet the requirements of both workers and management, you will find that there are plenty of opportunities for advancement in supervisory and managerial work.

OPPORTUNITY IS CONTINUALLY POUNDING

Whoever said "Opportunity knocks but once" didn't mean the managerial field of today. Opportunity doesn't knock once or twice or a dozen times but keeps up a continuous pounding that is unheard only by those who refuse to hear. For the higher positions industry needs supervisors with the ability to provide effective leadership for people who have come to expect much of management and its representatives.

Promotions go to the person whose record need not be qualified by a remark such as "He's all right but won't take full responsibility." One poor leadership quality, a bad attitude, for instance, may cause you to be passed over when a new and interesting assignment is open. But if you can improve yourself even a small amount in each leadership quality that workers and management expect, it may be enough to place you head and shoulders above the supervisor who sees no need for betterment.

WHAT MANAGEMENT WANTS

Eight qualities that determine supervisory ability are listed on the rating sheets used by several leading companies in periodically checking the efficiency of their supervisors:

1. Ability to develop an organization
2. Personal leadership
3. Ability to plan work
4. Technical knowledge
5. Cooperation in executing company policies
6. Judgment and decision
7. Acceptance of responsibility
8. Constructive and independent thinking

There are time-tested ways in which you can improve in each of the qualities that management expects you to have. The suggestions that follow are not the ideas of a few people but represent the combined experience of successful supervisors, industrial-relations men, and psychologists.

Ability to Develop an Organization

A supervisor's value is proportionate to the usefulness of the group of people whose efforts he directs. Ability to establish and maintain an effective organization that meets current needs and readily adapts itself to changing requirements is a first essential for every supervisor or executive.

Check your past judgment in selecting men to fill jobs. If

performance has measured up to expectations, you may find some good rules for the future; if not, ask where the man failed, where you failed, and guard against repeating the mistake. Analyze the jobs performed by your group in order to provide a basis for building a well-balanced complete organization. Study the aptitudes and abilities of each team member to be sure the abilities represented are well adapted to routine production and, whenever possible, to extraordinary requirements. Since requirements continually change, however, you must look ahead to next week, next month, and next year. Can your organization adapt itself to the new situations that it must face?

Personal Leadership

Personal leadership in developing subordinates to maximum efficiency, enthusiasm, and teamwork gives a team the extra punch that produces recognizable results.

So essential is personal leadership to good supervision that some supervisors, well equipped in this respect, have compensated for deficiencies in other factors. The term "leadership," though broad and hard to define, involves selling, planning, and teaching. It's necessary to *sell* yourself to your team; to win both respect and friendship by your actions and attitudes. *Sell* also the aims and ideals of your own organization and company to develop an enthusiastic spirit. *Plan* the team's work in such a way that you are pointing out a path to follow. *Teach* team members the things they need to know, developing the fullest potentiality of each one. Be everything you expect them to be: in enthusiasm, in loyalty, in hard work, in courtesy.

Ability to Plan Work

Fiery enthusiasm in a team is ill spent unless the supervisor has ability to analyze and schedule routine and emergency work with dispatch and efficiency and with a long-range viewpoint.

Although all workers are expected to do some advance thinking, planning is essentially a supervisory function. A small amount of time spent by you in planning or advance thinking on supervisory problems is well repaid when the time comes for a job to be done.

Outline the goals and activities of your entire group on a long-range and day-to-day basis. Then plan each job, step by step, from assignment to completion. But don't forget to plan your personal time and activities so that you can discharge all your duties without neglecting to do things (including long-range planning) expected of you by workers and management. Simplify and systematize all routine operations so that time is saved each day and week and month.

Remember, too, that supervisors are often made or broken by the way they handle special assignments—a rush job or one that's highly important. If you have your routine work under control, you can do a bang-up job in completing the special assignment.

Technical Knowledge

So that he will never have to apologize to his team or to management, a supervisor needs adequate knowledge for present work and capacity to gain additional knowledge for new and more important work.

READ ON STREETCARS

Those who know only last year's methods are often out of date. Even if you're an "old dog," you can still learn new tricks. Set aside a definite time for increasing your knowledge by reading technical journals and books. One-half hour a day for a year is equal in time to 3½ work weeks; 1 hour a day equals 7 weeks of 8-hour-a-day study. Minutes are precious; read on streetcars, while waiting for dinner or an appointment. Round out your education by enrolling in evening classes, by attending worthwhile lectures, by participating in the activities of professional societies.

Cooperation in Executing Company Policies

A supervisor must understand, explain, and secure adherence to company policies and procedures, suggest procedures for making them more effective.

Be genuinely interested in and thoroughly familiar with your department and company. Know the approved policies and the reasons behind them. Attempt sincerely to apply these policies in your group whether you favor them or not. If you disagree with a policy, it is more profitable for you to make a constructive suggestion than to indulge in futile griping. Place the good of the organization above your own selfish, immediate interests; it pays in the long run.

Above all, don't keep your men in the dark. Help them to understand every phase of company policy that affects them. If you can't explain fully, find out the answers.

Judgment and Decision

To keep his team "clicking" smoothly, a supervisor must exercise sound judgment and make prompt, effective decisions.

As a basis for sound judgment, be completely informed on the problems of your workers and management and on those that face you in the management of your group. Study these problems from every possible viewpoint. Dig deeply for all related facts. Classify and arrange the facts and turn them over in your mind until a complete analysis has been made. When you think you have the answer, don't jump to the conclusion that it is the correct one just because it sounds good. Test your solution thoroughly. Try the "other fellow's shoes" method. What decision would you make if you were in the boss's shoes? How would you accept that decision if you were in the worker's shoes? What would you think if you were another worker looking on? How will your decision affect accounting? engineering? manufacturing? sales? customers? If you have gone through this reasoning process without skipping any steps or allowing yourself to be influenced by your personal feelings or preconceived notions, you are ready to crystallize your decision.

Often you are expected to make a speedy decision without time enough to make a detailed study of the problem. Your ability to exercise sound judgment in making such decisions is enhanced if you have become thoroughly familiar with company policies and practices.

Acceptance of Responsibility

A real supervisor or executive willingly assumes full responsibility for successful completion of work supervised.

Avoid leaning too heavily on the boss, and don't be a "yes" man. If two people in an organization always agree, one of them is unnecessary. It could be you.

Be sure you have a definite, clear-cut outline of your duties and responsibilities; then seek added responsibilities that make you more valuable to the company. Be willing to take more blame for failures than you do praise for successes.

Constructive and Independent Thinking

Ability to originate and develop ideas intelligently and to make constructive suggestions and improvements is one of the most important factors in good supervision.

You would hardly be satisfied with the job you have done, if at the end of a year the best you could say was, "Well, the operation is no worse than it was when I started." The progress of your group and company depends on the development of new ideas, new methods, new goals, based on constructive and independent thinking. Thinking independently is refusing to be tied down to past or present methods and policies. Thinking constructively takes into consideration established precedents and weighs the advantage of departing from them against the value to be derived from a new idea. Constructive thinking is disciplined thinking, directed along channels defined by overall and immediate objectives of a group, a department, or a company.

When you have a bright idea, define clearly the value that it will bring to the group or the company. Then scout around a little more and see if the same value can be obtained with a change that is simpler or less radical. You will find that critical analysis of your own ideas will reduce criticism on the part of those to whom you have to sell them and will enable you to get results more quickly.

WHAT WORKERS WANT

Why do people work?

Day in and day out, some 60 million people in the U.S. put in 8 or 9 or 10 or more hours of work, some of it very difficult or disagreeable.

Do they do this solely because they want the money they receive? Or are there other reasons?

It is obvious that wages received are a direct reason why most of us work. But this is true only because money buys us satisfaction in the form of both the necessities and luxuries of life and because it is tangible evidence of recognition and a source of personal pride. Wages, however, cannot buy or measure the satisfaction received in licking a tough job or in seeing the product of one's ingenuity and effort take useful form. Nor can wages entirely compensate for lack of satisfaction with working conditions, personal relationships on the job, or living conditions outside the job.

The total satisfaction a person obtains from his job is the true yardstick of its value to him. Total job satisfaction depends, not only on the money received, but on satisfactions that result from the attitude and efforts of the worker himself, his fellow employees, his supervisor, and his company. It may be expressed as a formula:

(Total job satisfaction)	=	(Satisfaction from money)	+	(Satisfaction added by worker and fellow employees)	+	(Satisfaction added by supervisor)	+	(Satisfaction added by company)

The *plus satisfactions*, above and beyond that obtained from wages, may take the form of such things as pride in work,

WAGES ARE A DIRECT REASON

congenial fellow workers, pleasant surroundings, good working conditions, good supervision, opportunities for training and advancement. These things, many of which are controlled or influenced by the supervisor, are incentives that lead to efficiency since they determine how hard an employee is willing to work and how well he does his assignments.

The supervisor who wants to get top production from his team helps each worker individually achieve at least some of the *plus satisfactions*. He endeavors to eliminate or overcome *minus quantities* or *dis*satisfactions which result from lack of friendly encouragement, from unsuitable work assignments, from lack of friends in a strange community, or from similar causes.

The supervisor is able to influence the satisfaction added by the worker's attitude and that of the rest of the team, but he cannot appreciably reshape the personalities brought by employees to the job. Likewise, the front-line supervisor cannot do more than interpret with understanding the attitude of his company.

Modern companies have done wonders in employee relations in recent years by introducing personal services, pension plans, training programs, and the like. These are provided, not out of the "goodness" of somebody's heart, but because those who run the companies realize that these things add to job satisfaction and mean greater efficiency. They are meant to provide added satisfaction, not to take the place of intelligent supervision and effective leadership.

It is important that a supervisor know what specific job satisfactions are sought by each member of his team. He can then take steps to provide these incentives and use them in producing more and better work.

For a listing of what people want, we turn to an expert who makes it his business to know public opinion—Elmo Roper, conductor of Fortune's Public Opinion Poll, which has accurately forecast many local and national elections.

Mr. Roper states that people want four things from their jobs:

1. Job security (the security that comes from full employment at reasonable wages)
2. Chance to advance
3. "Just to be treated like people"
4. Feeling of dignity and responsibility[1]

The last three items depend, in a large degree, on things the supervisor does. If he satisfies the employee in the three desires over which he has considerable control, many of his problems will be nonexistent. Even in the case of job security, the supervisor contributes something, since security depends on a person's

[1] From a paper presented at the Manpower Stabilization Conference, American Management Association, New York, Sept. 28–30, 1943.

ability, which is often determined by the extent of his training and the opportunities for development. As a practical means of improving yourself as a supervisor, check to see what extra

CHANCE TO ADVANCE

things you can do to satisfy each of these desires for each person who reports to you.

Chance to Advance

Ambition is a characteristic of people in many nations, but nowhere is it any more developed than in our own country. Americans have a burning desire to succeed and will exert a great deal of effort if they see a hope of bettering themselves.

In a survey by a national magazine some years ago, 89 per cent of those questioned replied that "opportunities for advancement, training, and education" was a major work incentive. This factor was in second place, nosed out only by "job security, insurance and savings plans, pensions," which led by a 1 per cent margin. It ranked far above such things as "hours of work," "vacations with pay," and "working conditions."

In a survey of engineering employees at The Glenn L. Martin

Company in 1943, "opportunity for advancement, training, education" was placed first among 12 reasons that would make them want to work for a company.

OPPORTUNITIES FOR TRAINING

Surely, here is a desire which a supervisor can utilize to the utmost. The better jobs are going begging. They are awaiting those who are determined to become capable of filling them. In training his men for these opportunities, a supervisor can do these things:

Emphasize that advancement depends upon the way a person handles his present job; that is, on the quality of work, quantity of work, and the employee's attitude.

Point out the possible path of promotion, with emphasis on the next step.

Encourage outside study which will help the worker in doing better in his present job as well as provide a concrete basis for advancement.

Instruct the worker properly in the specific things he does repeatedly in his daily work.

Be sure no employee will have reason to feel he will be held back because his supervisor hoards competent man power or fears competition from his men.

In doing these things, the supervisor is helping himself as well as his men. Supervisors often miss a chance for promotion because they have not trained someone who can step into their shoes. On the other hand, many a supervisor has been promoted because he demonstrated his ability, not only to build an efficient organization but to develop men who contribute to the upbuilding of the company.

"Just to Be Treated Like People"

We return to Elmo Roper, who states that people want "what they call a 'friendly management,' and they want to see

FRIENDLINESS TO OVERCOME OPPOSITION

that friendliness reflected in a variety of ways—in working conditions, for instance, and in *all the little relationships between management and men* in the general workaday world. They want relationships that make them feel they are treated like people and that they have a genuine responsibility and a stake in the enterprise itself."

They want to realize that they are needed.

Since the supervisor is the representative of management and the person who has most contacts with employees, it is up to him to display the friendly interest that ranks so high as an employee desire.

It's no wonder that people seek this friendly interest. Working 8 hours or more a day, an employee spends a major part of his waking hours on the job. Hence, if his supervisor is sarcastic, disinterested, or otherwise unfriendly, the employee loses some of his zest for work.

Lacking a formula, the supervisor will probably be safe if he knows his workers well enough to appreciate their abilities and ambitions, then lets genuine friendliness take its natural course. Such an intimate knowledge of his workers' abilities will emphasize for the supervisor that each person is an individual

THE GOLDEN RULE MIGHT GET YOU INTO TROUBLE

case. Each has differences in personality, in education, in experience. Each will respond best to supervisory actions that are tailored to suit his individual situation.

As an example, let's take the general rule of "Give credit where credit is due," which is considered to be a good fundamental principle for supervisors to follow. Just what does it mean? Should a supervisor praise everything the worker does? Certainly not. Should a man have a raise for performing a difficult assignment? Perhaps he is paid well for doing just that kind of work and doing it the right way.

A new worker, or a sensitive one, or the introspective type may have a strong desire for frequent encouragement and praise.

The same treatment, however, may have no effect on the extrovert or "sales" type of person who is not so sensitive to the criticism or praise of his fellow men. And ill-considered praise would probably irritate the highly skilled worker who prefers recognition in the form of added responsibility and authority rather than fine words. Other individuals might become self-satisfied or conceited by too much commendation. Nine out of ten people, however, will react favorably to some form of praise, and the average supervisor is lax in making use of this incentive.

Perhaps it would not be well to follow too literally the Golden Rule, which states "Do unto others as you would have others do unto you." The rule might get you into trouble since your personality and that of the other fellow are probably quite different. Something that will spur you on to intensive effort may be the very thing that will annoy someone else with a different temperament. With this in mind, we humbly suggest qualifying the Golden Rule:

"Do unto others as you would have them do unto you *if you had the same personality and were in the same position as the other person.*"

Feeling of Dignity and Responsibility

Many people prefer to work in a professional field or in one of the so-called "white-collar" jobs because of the dignity and responsibility which they feel are associated with such work. To do this, they are often forced to accept smaller wages, another indication that wages alone do not fully satisfy the employee.

Dignity and responsibility can be a part of any job when the supervisor realizes their importance. Do you, as a supervisor, do these things which raise the employees' feeling of self-importance?

Make everyone feel that he is a vital member of the team and that his work is needed to make the team successful?

Encourage suggestions from employees and put them to use when they are feasible?

Delegate full responsibility for a definite piece of work to everyone, no matter whether it is a comprehensive job or just a detail?

Delegate authority commensurate with responsibility?

Give an employee opportunities to satisfy his creative urge to do something worth while?

Make every attempt to give the worker the kind of job in which he can excel?

Explain the final use of a job, the reasons why, so as to stimulate interest?

Inspire loyalty to the team and to the company?

Assign enough work so that no one has to sit around waiting for a job?

ASSIGN ENOUGH WORK

Plan your work, and know what you want, so that you do not need to change your mind when the employee has nearly completed an assignment?

In a nutshell, do you have a sincere appreciation of the importance of every member of your team and a modest evaluation of your own position?

2

Expect Much

THE "expect much" method is used by successful supervisors in building morale and securing results. Says LeRoy H. Kurtz of General Motors' public-relations department: "Morale results not from giving people something, but from *making proper demands upon them* to win the psychological rewards of achievement. As for direction and control, a tough but equitable discipline is a greater morale builder than the flabby partiality of uncertain generousness."

The recommended procedure is to set high standards and goals for your group, both in amount of work to be completed and in excellence of work. Let each individual know that you expect much, show your confidence in his ability to produce more than the minimum, and by good leadership make it possible for him to outdo himself.

A supervisor who expects little from his employees either lacks the competence necessary to leadership or lacks confidence in his employees' ability, which insults them and discourages them from doing their best. If, on the other hand, he expects a great deal, his confidence in them will be regarded as a compliment and his competence will be acknowledged by willing cooperation.

Just what should the supervisor expect?

There are four things which every supervisor should expect from his employees; if it's known that he expects them and if he provides the proper leadership, results should prove gratifying:

First, that they meet high quality and quantity standards, *and a little bit more.*

Second, that they maintain congenial personal and business

relations with all members of the group (and with other groups) and support spontaneous natural discipline.

Third, that they become increasingly useful to the group, taking on increased responsibility and requiring less supervision and instruction.

THE WISE SUPERVISOR EXPECTS MUCH

Fourth, that they offer helpful suggestions and make every attempt to solve problems and minimize difficulties rather than build them up and create trouble.

And a Little Bit More

There are certain standards of quality and quantity that cannot be relaxed without inviting inferior work in the future. As a supervisor, you should not be satisfied with the bare minimum. The team that's really a success produces work that meets the requirements and the little bit more that lifts it out of the mediocre class.

And how do you get these *plus* results? Certainly not by expecting fair or average work, nor by being easily satisfied, nor by relaxing standards so as to let inferior work get by.

Raise the standard for your team above the level of that required. Then, meet this goal with plenty of margin to spare. Expect high quality and quantity, and expect it at all times. But be sure you have been a good enough leader to provide your employees with everything they need to reach the objective.

If you expect much of your workers, they in turn will expect much of you. Your reaction will be the same as theirs. Meeting

DON'T BE TOO EASILY SATISFIED

their challenge will develop in you invaluable capabilities as a supervisor.

Good Personal Relations

Needless to say, congenial personal relations are to be expected as much as high production and quality. It is important to get a job done quickly and correctly, of course, but this is not enough. Employees should be expected to maintain harmony and good will, which ensure effective cooperation on future assignments as well.

Personal relations are usually good in a group when the individual desires of all members are satisfied—when each one realizes his part in promoting the team goal. The supervisor should be certain that the objectives of the group are clearly understood and that there is complete agreement on accepted procedures. If the supervisor does his job well, he should expect that all group members work together as a team for the good of all concerned. He must continually encourage employees to think in terms of the long-range interests of the company, the department, the group—interests that are really the same as those of individual members.

Discipline should be maintained, of course, but it should be fair and constructive—based not on fear of punishment, but on enlightened leadership which expects much, in terms of results; provides much, in terms of satisfaction for each individual on the team. When the supervisor expects much and the team is kept busy, many personal-relations problems vanish into thin air and there is less need for disciplinary measures.

Shouldering More Responsibilities

Some employees, more ambitious than the rest, demonstrate initiative in seeking added responsibility. Others have it thrust on them haphazardly, perhaps very abruptly. The ideal situation, however, is when the supervisor expects a worker to shoulder gradually increased responsibility and holds him accountable for results, making sure, of course, that instructions are clear and that the worker is able to secure everything he needs to complete his work.

Too many supervisors feel they must do a tough job themselves in order to get it just right. It is true that it may sometimes be less convenient and less dramatic for the supervisor to have one of his men do such a job than do it himself. Delegating work sometimes means more work for the supervisor, but it is work he should do, such as providing on-the-job training, outlining objectives, giving instructions, checking results.

Instead of taking authority and responsibility from his workers or holding them back, the wise supervisor makes each worker feel responsible for getting a job done and allows him to exercise the authority required to get it done.

Although the outstanding members of a group generally gain responsibility by assuming it or by training as understudies, much hidden talent remains to be uncovered in any group. Surprising results may come from placing additional responsibility on people who have been mediocre in past performance but who have shown ability along certain lines or in spurts. Such people can be encouraged to take on added responsibility by giving them a little more freedom, tapering off on instruction, giving them specific jobs to carry to completion, and allowing them to develop their own ideas.

Minimizing Difficulties

Nothing is more irritating to a supervisor than the trouble monger—the pessimist who always sees the black side of the picture and who emphasizes and exaggerates the problems and difficulties that confront a group. Problems aren't solved by

making them more complex, but by seeking simple, workable solutions. What you need to expect from employees is that they strive to solve the group's problems and minimize the difficulties facing the supervisor and the group.

You can encourage such an attitude by sincerely seeking the advice and assistance of group members. It often seems easier to lay down the law and insist on something being done your way—right or wrong. However, the *one best way* may be the method suggested by an employee. What a waste of ideas results when you fail to seek suggestions and assistance from employees. Perhaps a worker's ideas are not 100 per cent correct, but they may contribute to the final solution; at any rate, even if suggestions are not used, it enhances a worker's sense of belonging to the group and broadens his experience to get them off his chest and discover why they are not practical.

Each individual in your group wants to be considered an

important contributor to the group efforts; he may be willing to do a great deal more than standard in order to obtain recognition. Everyone wants to be on a winning team, one that produces results, but the chances are your team will be not much better than you expect it to be.

RATE YOUR TEAM

Try sizing up your team, using the following quiz. It will give you some idea about the efficiency of your group and

whether they are producing as much as you have a right to expect. Be sure to consider your group in relation to others doing similar work. Score on this basis:

Outstanding.............................. 5
Above average.......................... 4
Average.................................. 3
Below average.......................... 2
Poor....................................... 1

If the total score for the 20 questions that follow is near 100, either you're a starry-eyed optimist or your team is too perfect to live on this earth. If it's below 60, your group needs a shot in the arm.

Equip yourself with a pencil, and start scoring.

1. Do your group members have plenty of enthusiasm? Are they on their toes? [ ]

2. Do they keep busy at all times instead of "loafing" and "griping"? [ ]
3. Do they know the reasons behind the work they do, rather than just "grind it out"? [ ]
4. Are they quick in understanding your instructions? [ ]
5. Can you get results by *asking* them to do a job rather than commanding them? [ ]
6. How's their teamwork? Do they work well together? [ ]
7. Is their routine work kept in shape so that special jobs can be handled efficiently? [ ]
8. Does their work conform to standard practice? [ ]
9. Does the group make helpful suggestions? [ ]
10. Does each one carry his full share of the load? [ ]
11. Do they come to you for help when they need it? [ ]
12. Are they inclined to do their work without needless fretting and worry? [ ]
13. Are they improving themselves by means of night-school courses, lectures, outside reading? [ ]
14. Are they accepting responsibility for assigned work, rather than annoying you with every small detail? [ ]
15. Do they perform their jobs in a planned manner instead of hit or miss? [ ]
16. Is the quality of their work high? [ ]
17. Is the group vigilant in checking for errors? [ ]
18. Is your group careful in the proper use of material? [ ]
19. Do they get their work out on time? [ ]
20. Do they respond to constructive criticism and reprimands? [ ]

Add 'em up.................................. ________

It's Done with Mirrors

You've just rated your group, of course. But, what's more important, you've rated your own ability as a supervisor. For the qualities of a good leader are reflected in the people he leads.

With wise leadership, they'll be cooperative and efficient, producing work that's good in both *quality* and *quantity*. They will be imbued with *teamwork*.

LIST THOSE QUALITIES YOU WISH TO HAVE

If Benjamin Franklin were in your shoes, he'd probably consider this rating the same way he did his plan of life, which he describes in his *Autobiography*. First of all, he listed those qualities he wished to have. Then, he concentrated on improving himself in one quality each week. Every night he reviewed his actions during the day and, if he failed to measure up to his goal, he placed a black mark on a chart in his diary. Using this self-improvement plan Franklin eventually did all right for himself.

In contemplating your personal qualifications for supervisory leadership, remember that there are stumbling blocks, three of which have been enumerated by E. B. Wilson[1]:

"First, most executives [and supervisors] think they already are good leaders. They often are unaware both of their own shortcomings and of the possibilities for improvement.

"Second, they hesitate to admit they could improve, if they are aware of the fact, for fear of reflecting on their ability.

"Third, personal habits are hard to change and habits are at the root of the leadership problem. Even with the best of

YOU WON'T GROW WINGS OVERNIGHT

intentions, habits can be changed or adapted only after conscientious, continuous effort."

To get around these stumbling blocks, assume that you have room for improvement in every necessary leadership quality. (That's undoubtedly true.) Study yourself so as to unearth your faults. (Not easy, but needs to be done.) Admit your weaknesses. (That, in itself, shows strength of character.) Finally, make yourself change any personal habits that stand in the way of your development. (In forming new, more desirable habits, you must break completely away from the old ones, continually practice the new ones, and allow no exceptions.)

You'll make mistakes, of course, especially when you are tired or on a rush job. Perhaps you'll be quick-tempered, discourteous, prejudiced, or impatient. These mistakes are not trivial, but they can be put to work. Make every mistake teach you a lesson. Don't be discouraged if you fail to blossom out overnight with a halo, a pair of wings, and a brand-new personality. It takes time to develop leadership.

[1] WILSON, E. B., *Getting Things Done in Business*, McGraw-Hill Book Company, Inc., New York, 1942.

3

What Gets the Job Done?

MANY people say that enthusiasm is something everybody should have, like virtue. Others say it is dangerous, impelling Junior to kick his new football through a window and prompting Dodger fans to throw pop bottles at umpires. Too often, people try to substitute some ersatz baloney which they call enthusiasm for hard work, sound planning, or intelligent direction.

What is the *real* enthusiasm we can put to work in industry? You can't put your hands on it. You can't requisition it and install it in your department. But when a group is imbued with enthusiasm, quality and quantity are up, and the little but important things necessary to speed and accuracy are done without constant reminders. People get to work on time, or before, and don't stampede at quitting time. They perform tough jobs cheerfully. They make constructive suggestions. They are aggressive. They cooperate.

When enthusiasm is lacking, production slows down, "housekeeping" gets sloppy, rumors are rampant, people request transfers, minor gripes mushroom into major grievances, dissatisfaction with wages and ratings becomes unreasonable, petty jealousies flare into open antagonisms, and an important unit in production is knocked out.

What can a supervisor do when he sees that his group needs a straight shot of enthusiasm?

Give Yourself Something to Be Enthusiastic About

Back of every group with real job enthusiasm is a supervisor who radiates it himself. A cheerful but businesslike attitude, an

ENTHUSIASM IS CONTAGIOUS

enthusiastic voice, an eager manner in tackling tough assignments—all are as catchy as measles.

Some supervisors have this enthusiasm naturally. Others may take a tip from Shakespeare, "Assume a virtue if you have it not."

One way to develop your enthusiasm is to get to know your job and your workers. Know why your company is going places. Know why your department is indispensable to the company. Study the individuals in your group. What are their abilities, ambitions, and potentialities? What qualities in each individual can you honestly respect and admire? Study the individuals in relation to each other. Note how they cooperate, and consider new ways to achieve teamwork.

Write these things down in black and white. Not only does it give you a sound, intelligent, realistic basis for being enthusiastic, but the mere act of making a study of your group and the individuals in it generates enthusiasm in you, their supervisor.

With this done, list specific things that can be done to improve the group. Healthy gripes should never scare anyone. It takes only one step to turn them into constructive suggestions and actions. As improvements are made, enthusiasm builds up.

If your study doesn't convince you that your group is, or can be, the "best damned outfit" in the country, do something about it *today*.

Having developed your own enthusiasm, your next step is to transmit it to your group and to each worker in the group. There are two general rules: (1) Give the individual something to be enthusiastic about; (2) give the group something to be enthusiastic about.

Give Each Man Something to Be Enthusiastic About

To build enthusiasm, use the best abilities of each worker. Encourage him to develop his abilities by evening classes, reading, and lectures so that eventually he may be upgraded. And be sure he is rewarded by the security, opportunities, recognition, and sympathetic treatment for which he is striving.

One successful supervisor says,

"After completely analyzing the abilities of each worker, I know more definitely what assignments to give him. In an unfamiliar job, one that doesn't suit him, he'll produce only fair results. But give him a job that he's fitted for by aptitudes, training, and experience, and he shines by comparison.

"I let each man know just where he fits into the general scheme, and just why we need his best efforts. He realizes he's not just a number on a social security card, but a vital part of a vital group.

"Treated as an individual, he responds as an individual, not as a robot or mechanical man."

Another way to generate enthusiasm in an individual is to tell him the purpose and background of a job. "Know-why," says Alfred H. Sinks in *The Reader's Digest*, "is the shortest, surest path to the *know-how* that turns out products faster. . . .

"Workers who *understand* their jobs don't get bored and spend their time griping; they don't quit or stay away from work except for the most urgent reasons.

TRAINEE IN STRANGE NEW WORLD

"To many trainees the factory is a strange, alarming new world. Know-why helps make it familiar and friendly, and the chance to keep on learning new things fills this new world with excitement and variety. The worker sees, in his instructor's patient explanations, evidence that the management is interested in *his* working problems. . . ." He returns that interest with an enthusiasm which keeps finished goods tumbling faster off the production lines.

If a worker has made a good suggestion or has done an excellent job, he deserves recognition. Praise him publicly. Recognition of work well done can also be made on periodic merit-rating sheets if used by your company. It's important that such appraisals be honest and accurate, since they serve as a basis for salary progress. Though a deserved pat on the back goes a long way in building enthusiasm, giving proper credit doesn't call for flattery.

Just as important as giving credit when credit is due is intelligent, objective criticism of work that is not up to standard. Criticism must be made privately and on an impersonal basis. Damn the job, not the person. In the Army an officer may curse *at* a man—never curse the man.

Just as the young boy with a lawn to mow after school keeps out of trouble, the worker who is kept busy has no time for complaining, gossiping, spreading false rumors. Certain types of assignments, such as house cleaning, preparation of progress charts, or collection of data that will save time on future jobs, can be used by supervisors to fill slack periods.

Often there is much routine work that has to be done. Though usually monotonous, routine work is made somewhat more interesting by stressing its importance or establishing a schedule to beat. Especially tough assignments can be made as *challenges* to the worker to use his abilities to the utmost.

But the worker should be considered not only as an individual but as a member of a team. The successful supervisor is the one who can weld a variety of widely different people into a unified, cooperative group.

Give Your Team Something to Be Enthusiastic About

The supervisor is the only one who can effectively develop the all-important "We can do it" spirit. This is the spirit that enabled a Russian military and civilian army to hold Stalingrad,

DON'T "HOG" THE GLORY

the spirit that routed the Axis all over the globe. It's the spirit that drives a group of men to get out a rush job on time or ahead of schedule. No leader can develop it if he places a barrier between himself and his men and women. No leader has it if he says, "You do this job," and fails to carry his share of the load; or if he tells his boss when the task is completed, "Here's what *I* did last week." A supervisor never loses face by giving full credit to those who carry the brunt of the work. But he may lose face—and the spark of team enthusiasm—by grandstanding and "hogging" the glory.

Temperamental as they may seem, theatrical people have a motto that's as applicable in business as on the stage, "The show must go on." If the star is sick, an understudy is ready to step into her shoes. The manager himself has often stepped into minor roles at a moment's notice. Postmen have the same idea. Though it rains or snows or hails, "The mail must go through."

Such attitudes arise from pride in team accomplishments. The supervisor can stress the fact that when there's a rush job, his group will be able to do it. The work must be finished.

The world over, Americans are known for their vigorous, competitive spirit. Competition is as American as apple pie. This will to win shows itself in business struggles, in war, in contract bridge, in sports. It can also mean department A striving to do more and better work than department B.

Beating a schedule is an interesting way to develop the competitive spirit in any group, even though there is no group with which it can be compared. *There's a deep satisfaction* in getting out a difficult assignment on time, or a day early, and it's just what's needed to increase production. Day-by-day progress may be recorded by means of charts that will graphically show the group how the work is moving. Such charts are also a help to the supervisor in keeping his boss informed on progress.

It's sometimes necessary that everyone in a group be assigned to routine work. In these cases, all members must realize the need for doing this work in a hurry. Loafers on the job cannot be tolerated. Everyone should carry his full load of the group's work, not only for his own sake but for the morale of the entire team.

The team has a sound basis for enthusiasm if the supervisor fulfills his two-way responsibility by reporting progress to his men as well as to management. Employees are deeply interested in new developments, changes in plan that affect them. Much time is lost in idle speculation and gossip, enthusiasm is killed, if the group is not informed in advance about changes. They should be told the reason behind changes and be persuaded to accept a new order in the proper spirit.

A weak supervisor is sometimes tempted to make himself look good by tearing down his group, complaining about its weak points, suggesting that if it weren't for him nothing would be done. The strong supervisor backs his team to the limit. He stands for "My team right or wrong," making sure meanwhile that the team is *right*. If a mistake is made by the team, he insists that the team correct it.

There are many other ways in which a leader can inspire a group to peak performance—as many ways as there are supervisors. He must, for example, go to bat for his team on wage raises; avoid favoritism for certain team members; reward good work by giving preferred assignments; maintain an objective,

impersonal viewpoint; rebuff the bootlickers; always be frank and honest.

In a nutshell, real enthusiasm is based on thorough understanding and competence. It requires thinking, planning, perseverance, attention to details. It's made up of

Know-how, or the competence of each man for the job to which he is assigned

Know-why, a knowledge of why a job is important, an understanding of the job's background

Work, plenty of it, work that's interesting and challenging

Incentives in the form of pay, recognition, and advancement opportunities

Teamwork as shown by a "We can do it" attitude, a mutual respect in which supervisor and worker understand each other

Pride in company, department, group, and self

Real enthusiasm makes the group's output greater than the sum of the individuals' efforts, acting separately.

It stands up when the going is rough.

4

How to "Up" Quality

In most industrial organizations, there is a continual tug of war between high quality and high quantity of production. Neither quantity alone nor quality alone is sufficient. They go hand in hand in a smooth, hard-hitting organization that gets results. The supervisor therefore needs to keep one eye peeled on the accuracy of his team's work and the other on the speed with which it is done.

A supervisor, says Spriegel and Schulz,[1] must "make his men quality conscious by instilling in them a pride to produce and maintain quality. To do this, the supervisor must possess knowledge and leadership—a knowledge of what quality is, how it can be measured, controlled and produced, and leadership to develop in his men the skills to meet the standards set. . . ."

In creating and maintaining quality, it is recommended that the supervisor

1. Establish definite quality responsibilities for each team member.
2. Develop pride in high quality standards in his team.
3. Set an example by the quality of his own work.
4. Know standard procedure and impart this knowledge to his group.
5. Know and train his team to know the quality requirements for each type of work.

[1] Spriegel, William R., and Edward Schulz, *Elements of Supervision*, John Wiley & Sons, Inc., New York, 1942.

6. Study the errors made and take steps to correct the underlying causes.
7. Persistently follow up to be sure that the standards are not relaxed.

Definite Responsibilities

The supervisor is accountable for every member of his team—and this includes their errors as well as their good work. It is a responsibility he cannot evade. It is up to him to train his men and organize his team to obtain high quality work on a routine basis. The following are suggested as fundamental principles:

> Every supervisor an instructor in quality when a job is assigned
>
> Every worker a "checker" of his own work
>
> Every checker or inspector a double checker of all items
>
> Every supervisor a persistent "follow-upper"

Note that the supervisor is mentioned twice: first, as an instructor, who in giving out a job must have it well outlined, so he can present it in clear-cut fashion; second, as a "follow-upper" who makes a thorough check of major items and checking methods and who will not let a job leave his group until it is right.

Develop Pride in Quality

When a person develops an idea that's all his own, on his own time, he has a feeling of pride that makes him triple-check himself until everything is *just so.* To develop similar pride in each person on his team is the job of the supervisor.

In building up job pride, give the *reasons why* the work assignment is important and show the consequences if it is inaccurate. You can develop a spirit of competition by pointing to the record of a group noted for the excellence of its performance. You can appeal to their desire for approval by commendation of work well done. A fundamental rule for supervisors is that workers respond to praise more than to faultfinding. So, when you find it necessary to point out errors (as you should) sandwich the faultfinding in between recognition of portions of the work that are well done. Intelligent criticism is that which points out both good work (as an example to follow) and poor work (as something to avoid). Point out, too, that advancement is based on both quality and quantity of work.

Generally, a worker will assume *full* responsibility for quality only when he receives *full* recognition when it is accomplished. If you give your men credit for a job well done, they have more

TRY THE ENCOURAGEMENT OF PRAISE

reason for seeing to it that it is well done. But, if you take all the glory and the team knows it (as it will), you cannot expect top-notch results unless you send them to the movies and do the work yourself. It often pays to ask your workers for suggestions on improving quality and to put them in practice if feasible. Call your team together to get ideas on such improvements.

Set an Example

When sloppy work is done by the supervisor, he can hardly expect anything better from his team. They look to him as an example to follow. If he is unrelenting and uncompromising in his striving for quality, the rest of the group tends to fall in line. Consistency is important, too. If strict standards are the rule one day and anything goes the next, the discipline and morale of the group will be lowered and it will be difficult for the supervisor to convince his group that quality is really vital. One careless remark under pressure such as "Let 'er go and we'll hope it's right," may be picked up by the team and applied as standard practice.

Training in Correct Procedure

The value of training in reducing errors has been demonstrated at The Glenn L. Martin Company's engineering department in conferences in which typical supervisors explained the

DISCUSS THE PURPOSE OF A FORM

use of standard forms such as the drawing change notice and engineering job sheets to "learners" recruited from fellow supervisors. In using these forms, considerable difficulty had, from time to time, been reported because those filling them out did not have a true conception of their importance and eventual use. Too often, a seemingly trivial detail such as a model number was inaccurate. This did not seem important to the draftsman, who reasoned that "it should be obvious" to people further down the line. But, since all detail information called for on such forms is vital to somebody in engineering, production, tool design, manufacturing, or accounting, special attention needed to be paid to getting it entered correctly on the standard form.

In these training conferences the participating supervisors first discussed the purpose of a standard form, explained where it originated and what happened to it. The job of filling out the form was broken down into definite steps, complete with (1) the reason why for each step; (2) the source of information; and (3) those key points that ensure accuracy. Confronted with the necessity for really understanding a standard form and its purpose, the supervisors were able to do a better instruction job. Using similar methods, a supervisor can turn inexperienced personnel into more accurate workers.

When instructing your team in standard procedure, avoid the temptation to curse red tape. Red tape is simply a system composed of many standard forms and procedures which are necessary in a large organization where a great number of people must be able to obtain accurate information without the necessity for time-wasting personal contacts on routine matters. Calculus and mechanics are involved too, but a college engineering student spends 2 or 3 hours daily for an entire academic year in learning the system of differential, integral, and applied calculus. A fraction of this time spent by a worker in studying a standard form or procedure should enable him to use it properly and thus make it possible for others to utilize the information quickly and correctly.

SHOW HIM WHERE AND HOW

Training in Quality Standards

Training in quality standards is perhaps best done right on the job at the time a worker is given an assignment. It's especially important to train the new worker in these standards as soon as he enters the group and before he lapses into sub-standard performance. Show him where and how to get the information, but have him look it up himself so it will stick. Both the supervisor and the workers need to be thoroughly familiar with the manuals, catalogues, and reports that give the required quality standards.

Study Causes and Cures for Errors

Behind every error, there must be a cause. Sometimes errors are blamed on a generality such as carelessness. But what caused the carelessness? Perhaps a man had distressing personal

UNEARTH THE REAL REASON

troubles and so did not have his mind on his work. The alert supervisor will, without being nosey, attempt to unearth the *real reason* for the carelessness, then take steps to correct the condition.

Some supervisors have found it desirable to keep records of errors that cause a job to "bounce back" to the group. Such a diary will tell you which errors recur most frequently and will enable you to double-check danger items and provide means of preventing their recurrence.

Wherever an error is made, it is preferable to have it corrected by the one who made it. This not only calls attention to the mistake but demonstrates the extra work involved in its correction. The error then becomes a practical lesson, which shows that it takes less time to do a job right in the beginning. This may not always be possible because the original worker may be assigned to another job, or because necessity for meeting a schedule seems to call for correction by a higher rated man. In these cases, however, the supervisor loses a golden opportunity for an effective type of on-the-job training.

The following are some common causes of errors, together with suggested methods of preventing them.

Errors—Causes and Cures

Causes	*Cures*
1. Worker "in a fog" about what he is supposed to do.	1. Supervisor must give clear-cut, definite instructions. For inexperienced people, break job down into steps that are easy to follow.
2. Doesn't have sufficient job knowledge.	2. Recommend evening classes, study of company manuals, or other sources of standard methods, processes, and procedures. Show worker where to find correct practice whenever he encounters a new problem.
3. Not familiar with procedure of your specialized group.	3. Be patient. Take time to explain problems fully as they arise.
4. Doesn't know quality standards.	4. Requires familiarity with company manuals and other references (or informal practices, whether established by directive or precedent). Insist that worker look up the standard practices in-

Causes	*Cures*
	stead of guessing. Warn him of the pitfalls.
5. Information on proper procedure obsolete.	5. Keep systematic files of all memoranda that explain proper procedure. Discuss changes in practice with group as often as needed.
6. Not familiar with requirements of other departments.	6. More contacts with these departments as a routine on-the-job training procedure.
7. Just doesn't care.	7. Find out why. Then try to improve attitude.

JUST DOESN'T CARE

Causes	*Cures*
8. "Impossible" schedules.	8. Make thorough investigation before giving promises or estimates.
9. Interrupted work.	9. Plan the work. Break the job down so that, if necessary, you can interrupt it at a place where the job can be picked up again efficiently.
10. Taking things for granted.	10. Insist that everything be checked.

Causes	*Cures*
11. Thinks details are unimportant.	11. Show how the small errors can lead to waste of man-hours and material.
12. Failure to follow instructions.	12. Return job to worker for correction, pointing out difference between work as done and as required. Stress necessity for following instructions.
13. Failure to check own work.	13. Impress worker with necessity for giving each job a *final review* before releasing it.
14. Worker in position not suited to his abilities.	14. After giving him every chance to make good, suggest transfer if he is not successful.
15. Checker or inspector irritates people to point of not caring	15. Be sure checker or inspector is unyielding in his quality standards so as to be respected and, at the same time, kindly and genial.
16. Too much haste.	16. Show that *doing a job right the first time* saves man-hours and trouble.
17. Worries about personal problems.	17. Family? Housing? Debts? Health? Eyesight? (The personnel department may be of assistance.)

Persistent Follow-up

A supervisor cannot go through every step the worker has followed in performing a job; he should not have to duplicate the efforts of the checker or inspector. To keep quality high, however, there are certain checks a supervisor can make without duplicating effort or becoming too involved in detail. One method is *overchecking*, that is, detail checking of an occasional job that has already been checked, so as to be dead sure that standards are being upheld. *Spot checking* of items picked at random also indicates to some extent whether quality control is adequate. *First-job checking* gives excellent results. Be sure to check thoroughly the first job by a new man or the first job of a new type encountered by any man. This gives you an opportunity to establish proper work habits right at the start. Such checking pays big dividends in saving time and trouble on more important work later on.

5

Employee and Supervisory Gripes

Until we develop an industrial Utopia, employees will have certain gripes against their supervisors; the supervisors, in turn, will have faults to find with employees who violate rules and regulations. In the first case, the supervisor needs to reexamine his actions or those of management and take steps to adjust the grievance. In the second case, he needs to examine the actions of the employee and, when necessary, take disciplinary action to prevent recurrences of violations.

EMPLOYEE GRIPES AND GRIEVANCES

Call it a gripe. Call it a grievance. Call it a misunderstanding.

By any name, an employee grievance is something that can be demoralizing enough to lower drastically the output of your group.

Just what is a grievance?

An industrial-relations expert[1] says, "Anything about a

[1] Gardiner, Glenn, *How to Handle Grievances*, Elliott Service Company, New York, 1943.

man's job which irritates him or tends to make his working conditions unsatisfactory may be a grievance."

It may be expressed or silent; trivial or important; caused by the supervisor, fellow workers, or management. Quite often, one irritation does not constitute a grievance, but repetitive irritations do.

There is no such thing as an imaginary grievance, as far as the aggrieved is concerned. To him it is *real.* Remember that such a grievance may have as bad an effect on production as a just grievance.

There are dozens of causes of grievances. Avoid the following major ones and you are well on your way to having a contented group.

Causes of Grievances

Hastily prepared merit ratings or reports, verbal or written, dealing with employee performance

Issuing orders without reasons

Poor planning

Unfair handling of overtime

Withholding credit when due

Blaming workers unfairly

Ignoring complaints

Hard-boiled attitude

"High-hat" supervision

Lack of interest in workers

Bawling out workers in presence of others

Breaking promises

Uncomfortable working conditions

Unequal pay for equal service

Poor instructions that lead to mistakes

Use of threats

Stealing credit for worker's ideas

Ignoring or discouraging suggestions

Unfriendly fellow workers

Assigning men to jobs for which they are not suited

Too little work

Favoritism or semblance of favoritism

Two-faced attitude

Evasive answers to direct questions

Obstructing worker's opportunities

Griping

Griping is an old American indoor sport that allows people to let off steam and calls attention to undesirable situations.

LET 'EM BLOW OFF STEAM

Encourage your men to tell you their grievances. Caught early, a gripe may be corrected before it is built up into a major problem. It may be an important step in making real improvements in the supervision of your group.

Griping alone does not usually produce satisfactory results. However, griping with a constructive suggestion added is a horse of a different color.

Handling Grievances

Consider a gripe or grievance as a danger signal, comparable to the sign at the railroad crossing which cautions you to Stop, Look, Listen.

In handling a grievance, turn this safety motto around. Listen, Look, Stop.

Listen to the worker with a grievance, patiently, sympathetically, open-mindedly.

Look at the problem objectively, weighing *all the facts.*

Stop the causes behind the grievance promptly, or show that there is no cause for complaint.

Listen Patiently

When a man reaches the boiling point, it's wise to allow him to let off steam. A grievance that stays inside a person is inflated in size and can be much more serious than one that is brought out into the open.

Make it easy for a member of your group to come to you with his problems. Don't stare him into a retreat. Rather, place him at ease by friendliness and sincerity.

Listen with interest to his story. It vitally affects your standing as a supervisor. Let him do the talking so that you get the story straight. Ask him to repeat it so that you are sure you understand his viewpoint. If you think it will help, let him repeat it a third time. And don't think that by changing the subject you can make him forget. He won't.

Avoid the temptation to argue, interrupt, or jump to conclusions. You may be wrong and, even if you're dead right, it pays to listen.

Remember that it is your job to back up your men when they have just complaints. If you don't do this and they go over your head for justice, you lose their respect and that of your superior as well.

Look at Problem Objectively

A grievance is often based on emotion rather than logic. You must not be swayed by the personal feelings of the aggrieved nor by your own feelings. But you can't ignore his personal feelings.

Look at the problem objectively from all viewpoints—the worker, the management, other workers.

Get all the facts you can that bear on the problem. Interview other workers for their opinions, but differentiate between

GET THE REASON BEHIND THE REASON

opinions and *facts*. (However, in discussing problems with other employees, avoid betraying confidences or violating the right of personal privacy. Such actions provoke violent resentments.)

Keep in mind that there are often two reasons for a person's action: the one he gives and the real reason. Get the reason behind the reason. A good worker may gripe about his wages, but his real grievance may be that he hasn't been given due credit for an excellent job.

When you have secured all the facts from every source, weigh them carefully. Determine whether or not there is a real grievance or an imaginary one.

Stop Causes Promptly

If there is a real grievance, take action promptly as soon as you have made a decision. It's not good practice merely to agree with the complainer and pass the buck to someone else. That breeds disrespect.

Perhaps you cannot handle the grievance personally. But you can present the facts to your superior and point out the necessity for action.

If the facts show the complaint to be imaginary, a straightforward "no" is required. However, it is essential that you explain by giving the reasons behind it. Give a reasonable answer to a reasonable question. Admit errors that you have made. It will stamp you as a bigger man.

If the worker is wrong, make it easy for him to back down on his demand. Let him save face. Don't rub it in.

Before telling your decision to the complainer, however, ask yourself these questions:

"How will the action affect production? the worker? the remainder of the group?"

Profit by Mistakes

Even the best supervisors have occasionally failed to take cognizance of danger signals in their group and have noted the resultant disruptions of production and discipline. However, they have studied the causes and effects and have built up a mental filing system for quick reference when similar signals go up in the future.

Study the situation of each of your workers, and correct grievances before they occur or while they are small and harmless.

SPARE THE ROD AND SPOIL THE CHILD

Many a successful person has been reared in accordance with the motto "Spare the rod and spoil the child."

It may not have been good psychology, but our grandparents claimed it kept our fathers and mothers on the "straight and narrow."

No doubt these old-timers were somewhat strict. But how about our present-day supervisors in industry?

Some people say they are getting soft and ineffectual.

Whether or not this is true is a matter for argument. The important fact is that discipline is as necessary in an industrial "army" as it is in a military force. That doesn't call for bullying supervision, but a quiet, efficient, kindly forcefulness. It doesn't mean tough manners, but rather tough, decisive thinking and action.

Discipline simply means handling employees so that they will have, as far as work is concerned, good morals, good manners, good methods: *good morals* that mean conformity to what is honest, right, and proper; *good manners* that mean acting according to accepted customs; *good methods* that mean orderly work habits.

Discipline and morale go hand in hand. You can't forget discipline and expect to have good morale. Certain actions cannot be tolerated. Chronic lateness and absenteeism, loafing, insubordination, horseplay, dishonesty, disregard for rights of fellow workers—all are disastrous to morale.

Usually the supervisor himself must bear a major share of the blame for lax discipline, since discipline and morale are his responsibility. The chief mistakes made by a supervisor along this line are inconsistency in enforcing discipline; unfairness; partiality; laxness in devising and applying corrective measures; failure to recognize differences in individuals; failure to keep an eye on workers and their problems; a hypercritical attitude; and issuing orders impractical to enforce.

The old-fashioned idea of discipline was that crime must be punished. Today we feel that the important thing is to correct errors and prevent their recurrence. A supervisor must therefore have a constructive outlook rather than a desire merely to punish an offender.

Although it is desirable to point out errors and shortcomings, it is equally necessary to reward good work and give due credit for jobs well done. Mixing praise for good work along with constructive criticism of mistakes is an effective method of maintaining enthusiasm while performing an unpleasant disciplinary task.

"BULLYING" SUPERVISION

Promoting Discipline

There are three major ways in which a supervisor can promote discipline, according to Brannon:[1]

1. Insist upon neatness, cleanliness, and orderliness, both in work surroundings and in work habits.
2. Standardize procedures. Simplify, systematize, regulate work.
3. Give clear-cut instructions, and see that they are followed.

No matter how excellent the supervisor, however, a certain number of errors and violations of rules are bound to occur.

The best time to take action is after the first offense, when mild measures may prove very effective. If an employee discovers that he can get by with something, your organization is in danger. One offense is apt to lead to another, and you soon lose control of your group.

When you are taking action, make it prompt, firm, and effective. Be sure the worker admits he is wrong, that he sincerely

[1] Brannon, Jerald A. Foster, *Modern Industrial Leadership*, National Foremen's Institute, Inc., Deep River, Conn., 1942.

wants to avoid repeating the offense, and that he does not resent your action.

In applying the necessary discipline, it is common sense to start with the mildest forms and work toward the severest. Before taking any action, however, be sure of your ground.

> Have you the entire story about the case?
>
> Are you disciplining the person who is to blame?
>
> Is the disciplinary measure deserved?
>
> Does it suit the individual?
>
> Are you in a calm and collected mood, unswayed by anger or other emotions?
>
> Have you worked out a *corrective* action?

Plan your discipline so that your employees will respect you and company regulations, and, at the same time, like you enough to work vigorously toward a common goal under your leadership.

Correcting Errors

Correction of errors is a mild form of disciplinary action but can be very effective if done immediately. The purpose is to prevent a recurrence of the error or offense, not to fix the blame. Focus your attention on the error, not on the man who is responsible.

Errors may result from lack of skill or knowledge, poor working habits, or carelessness, or they may be unavoidable. Sometimes the supervisor is responsible, especially if instructions have been hasty, conflicting, or confusing.

Errors may often be corrected by simply watching a man at work or by asking questions about a job. If necessary, point out the error in kindly fashion or show him how to do the job right. A worker respects a supervisor who is a practical man, fully capable of performing a job in a workmanlike fashion.

Quite often, it will pay a supervisor to have a friendly talk with the man who continually makes errors or whose work is below the standard. So important is the necessity for constructive criticism in such cases that the subject is discussed in detail in the next chapter.

Reprimands

Repeated trivial offenses and the more serious ones call for some sort of reprimand, which can range from a mild rebuke to a "bawling out." Its purpose is to make the offender agree that he has made a mistake and resolve to correct his actions.

Once you are sure of your facts, don't beat around the bush. Arrange a *private* session with the offender. Get to the point

BE CALM AND COLLECTED

quickly. Keep calm and collected, yet remain firm. Avoid becoming angry or starting an argument.

Carry the reprimand as far as it is needed, but be sure you are improving morale, not destroying it. A thin-skinned person often gets as much good out of a mild reproof as a hard character does from an old-fashioned dressing down. However, suit the severity of the reprimand to the seriousness of the offense. You don't have to make any threats. Chances are the employee knows whether you can recommend a transfer or discharge, whether or not you can carry it out yourself without the approval of your supervisor.

Alfred M. Cooper[1] says, "A good supervisor can reprimand in such a manner that the employee understands exactly where he or she has transgressed, and also leave the offender with the feeling that the reprimand was deserved. The subordinate knows, too, that unless the offense is repeated, nothing more will ever be said on the subject."

[1] Cooper, Alfred M., *How to Supervise People*, McGraw-Hill Book Company, Inc., New York, 1941.

It's relatively easy to bawl a person out and tell him what is wrong. But your job is to rebuild the employee and make him more valuable. Attempt to uncover the causes for work failures and violation of rules so as to prevent a second offense. Encourage workers to consider a reprimand as a lesson and a challenge to do better. Guide them in the formulation of corrective actions.

After your discipline job is complete, make every effort to be friendly with the employee and show him you hold no grudge. By all means, don't let him go away angry.

Nagging is out. It will make you as unpopular as a nagging husband or wife. It's a confession that you have failed in your reprimand.

True test of your effectiveness: Have you improved morale?

Transfers and Discharges

Infraction of serious rules, malicious damage, outright insubordination—these call for more serious treatment.

Passing the buck to another supervisor by transferring an employee is the favorite trick of a weak supervisor. Transfers are

effective measures only when a clash of temperaments has occurred or when an employee will be engaged in more suitable work in a new job.

Discharges are very serious affairs. They concern not only you, the supervisor, but your superiors and personnel representatives as well. Your role is presentation of all the facts in the case to the best of your ability.

Whenever a man is discharged, there are two failures involved: failure of the man to make good and your failure as a supervisor to develop him into a successful employee. Discharge is the last step in administering discipline, to be used only after other measures have failed. If you are forced to this final step, it might be well to review the case and your method of handling it at each step. Even though this will not affect the present situation, it may help you in the future.

6

Man to Man

MANY industrial supervisors today are good leaders and give every consideration to the needs and desires of those who work for them. They sincerely try to follow the principles of good job relations.

They believe in giving credit where due.

They want employees to know in advance about changes that will affect them.

They feel that each worker should be used to the best of his ability.

They want employees to know how they are getting along.

And they realize that people are different, that each is an individual who requires special handling.

Some supervisors, however, make the mistake of pampering their employees, keeping them happy at any cost. They use kid gloves in handling men but omit the firm, iron hand. They are too weak to do something about the unsatisfactory employee—the one who is below par.

The problem has been summed up by A. L. Kress[1] in this way: "Unfortunately there is not enough constructive criticism given to the man who is not doing a good job. Too many persons in supervisory positions do not have the guts to sit down and talk calmly and frankly with a man about his shortcomings. We are apt to critcize our subordinates to others, even to their fellow workers (which is a grave mistake), but we seldom tell the man himself, face to face, where he is falling down. It seems

[1] Kress, A. L., *Foremanship Fundamentals*, McGraw-Hill Book Company, Inc., New York, 1942.

so much easier to evade issues of this kind, but they have a way of catching up with us sooner or later.

"If you are to be a builder of men, you must analyze every man's performance in terms of concrete things such as quality, quantity, job knowledge, cooperation and try to see what it is that prevents him from doing the most effective job. When you

have done that and are sure you have put your finger on the reasons, sit down and have a friendly man-to-man talk."

Most supervisors have talks with their employees. But they are not man-to-man or heart-to-heart. The supervisor kids the employees by not being frank, and he also kids himself. Here's a case in point:

One supervisor called in a member of his group and said (as accurately as we can report it), "A job opening has developed in another group. We believe you can handle it excellently, and are recommending your transfer."

After hearing the details, the somewhat startled employee asked, "Isn't my work all right? My merit rating is high, and I'd like to stay where I am."

Continuing the "man-to-man" talk, the supervisor explained that the employee's work was excellent, but that the new job would be better suited to him and offered increased possibilities of promotion.

With his morale built up in this way, the employee took the new job, worked at it for a number of weeks, but didn't measure up to the "inflated" recommendations given him by the previous supervisor. When his poor work was pointed out to him, he immediately asked to have his old job again.

The matter was discussed with the previous supervisor, and these facts were revealed:

The man had also done poor work in his previous job.

The transfer was made in order to get rid of him.

The previous supervisor did not want him back.

Weasel to Man

The first supervisor had had, not a man-to-man talk, but a weasel-to-man talk with the employee. He was guilty of these violations of the principles of good supervision:

Deliberate falsification of the employee's merit rating

Passing the buck on a supervisory problem by means of a transfer

Giving an unmerited recommendation of the employee

Failure to criticize the work of the employee constructively

The supervisor had failed to let the employee know how he was getting along. He had overlooked inferior work and had even praised it by means of high merit ratings. Thus his problem, which might have been helped by constructive criticism, had grown until his only apparent alternative was to get rid of the employee.

What should the supervisor have done?

Obviously, a logical first step would have been to analyze honestly the work and attitudes of the employee.

Know the Employee

There are many ways of analyzing an employee. One is by conscientious evaluation of each quality required, preferably on a standard merit-rating form, with a standard job description used as a yardstick. Each item on the rating form of the employee mentioned above should have been studied carefully. Honest rating would have revealed his substandard performance.

Next step would have been to ask *why*.

Was the employee suited to his job? Did he lack experience or training? Did he have personal troubles that affected his work? What specific actions and attitudes demonstrated his shortcomings?

The supervisor should also have noted whether or not the methods of supervision were at fault. Had he done everything possible to change the employee from a substandard to a satisfactory worker?

Armed with a thorough knowledge of the employee, the supervisor would have been able to decide on methods for improvement.

After considering the attitude of the employee and choosing the right approach, he would be prepared for a friendly man-to-man talk.

Man to Man

There are several rules to keep in mind in talking with an employee man to man.

Be fully prepared as mentioned above.

Open in a friendly manner.

Mutually develop the problem in concrete terms.

Work together in solving it.

Decide mutually on *specific* actions.

Remain friendly.

Follow up on results.

Be sure your man-to-man talk takes place at a time when both you and the employee can give the problem your full atten-

tion, and at a time when you both will find it easy to be friendly and cooperative.

Open your talk in a friendly manner, but be sure your approach suits the individual. Sometimes you will want to come to the point immediately, especially in dealing with people who know how to take criticism. Many times, however, you will find it desirable to point out both the good and bad characteristics of the employee—leading into his shortcomings gradually. Checking his efficiency with him, point by point, gives you an opportunity to do this without sounding artificial or insincere.

Recognition of the good work he has done is not merely to make him feel happy but to emphasize the right way to do things and stimulate his efforts to do better work so that he can secure additional recognition. Pointing out his bad work and showing how he can improve gives him a sound basis for working toward such recognition.

Avoid generalities in favor of specific illustrations of what you mean. It's not wise to say that he is too careless or that he does not cooperate. Mention particular errors that resulted in wasted time on a job. Show that, by failing to work hard on a particular assignment, he held up completion of a job that many people were anxiously awaiting.

Let the employee do much of the talking. Most likely he will feel better about explaining his poor qualities himself. However, be sure he recognizes that he does have a problem and that it is necessary for him to improve.

If the employee will frankly admit that he has a problem, the battle is half won, and if you have permitted him to do plenty of talking in developing the problem, you can be sure he will be more cooperative in doing something about it.

Having carefully studied the problem, you will have one or two solutions in mind before the interview starts. However, you will be better off if you allow the employee to suggest what he should do to correct the situation. Encourage him to propose one or more plans of action, which can be combined with your own suggestions or modified by mutual agreement.

These suggestions for improving his shortcomings should be specific. Show that he can prevent errors by carefully reviewing his own work. Show how he can save time by checking doubtful points with you or some other member of the group. Show how certain evening courses or home study can enable him to equal or exceed the requirements for his job.

Do not conclude your talk until the employee has a sincere desire to correct his shortcomings and believes he has a practical plan for doing so. Let him know that you have confidence in his ability to make good and that you will do whatever you can to help him. Let him know also that you are friendly, and be sure you display a friendly attitude in your contacts with him after you have completed your talk.

Your job is not finished, of course, simply because you have had the courage to criticize the employee. *Talk alone will not do the job.* It is up to you to check his future actions and attitudes and be certain that the talk has accomplished what you intended.

At some future time, you may want another friendly heart-to-heart get-together during which you can discuss his progress and recognize any improvements in his work or attitude.

You'll find that a man-to-man talk is one of the most effective supervisory tools you have. True, it takes courage to sit down with an employee and tell him what's wrong. It's easier to let such things slide and throw more work in the direction of qualified employees (even though this is unfair to them).

But constructive criticism is one of your major obligations as a supervisor. It marks the difference between a capable, experienced leader and one who should be demoted to a position that does not call for leadership responsibilities.

7

Orders—Supervisory Tools

GIVING orders appears to be one of the simplest jobs that confronts a supervisor. However, the thinking behind an order and the manner in which it is given determine the attitude of the worker and the speed and efficiency with which the work is carried out.

A single order is really three different orders:

1. What you think you say
2. What you do say
3. What the other person thinks you say

Between your interpretation and that of the other person may be a wide gap. It is your duty to narrow that gap so that a clear-cut understanding results. Until orders are thoroughly understood, you have not done your job.

Orders are the tools that enable you to get an assignnent under way. First of all, you want to get a specific job done, but you may have secondary objectives as well. Do you want to increase cooperation? improve discipline? express or inspire confidence? develop new methods? hold a worker to strict accountability? get a disagreeable job done? reduce your supervisory worries? instruct a new employee? No matter what your aims, you can shape your orders to help you get the results you want.

To Increase Cooperation

When you want something from a person who is on an equal footing, it is, of course, necessary to make a courteous request. And therein lies the key to securing cooperation from those who work for you as well. Make your orders be requests and you'll get a little more cooperation, more work done, less friction. It's no harder to phrase your order "How about doing this . . . " or "Would you find out . . . " and it's the friendly way of making assignments.

A request melts (or partly melts) the hard-boiled man. It puts the nervous, irritable worker at ease. It doesn't offend a touchy, sensitive person or an older man or a fellow supervisor. It enables you to get a difficult job done the way you want it. The request is also desirable in giving orders to a new employee, one who is untrained, or the person who is deeply interested in his work.

The first time you reprimand an employee, it's better to *ask* him to correct the mistake rather than to give a command. Your reprimand calls attention to the error and makes the employee admit that he is wrong; the "request to correct it" adds the friendliness that keeps him on your side.

To Secure Discipline

If most of your orders are requests, the occasional command will stand out emphatically. It will serve as a disciplinary measure for those who are lazy or indifferent or careless or dis-

IF YOU EMPHASIZE EVERYTHING

obedient. It may even stop for a while those who are chronic gripers and talkers. When speed is highly important, the industrial supervisor can drive the fact home by changing from the usual request to the occasional command.

Remember, however, that a command is a means of getting emphasis and that, if you emphasize everything, you actually emphasize nothing. Used consistently, the command antagonizes the average person and infuriates the touchy or hard-boiled types. Used sparingly, the command can help improve the discipline of the team or get an emergency assignment completed quickly.

To Express or Inspire Confidence

The implied or suggestive order stimulates employees to use their own judgment. It is an expression of confidence and an invitation to a man to take on added responsibility and use his own initiative. It is just as valuable, therefore, in giving assignments to a dependable employee as it is undesirable in the case of those who are inexperienced or unreliable.

There is a middle group of employees who have not proved their worth but who demonstrate potential ability. You can inspire confidence in them by showing that you trust their judgment. Perhaps they have been checking certain decisions with you for some time, and you find yourself in agreement in practically every case. This is an indication that they can safely be tried out "on their own" in such matters. Gradual increase of responsibilities is an effective way to develop high-grade employees.

To Develop New Methods

In developing new methods or new designs, it may be preferable that a worker have a fresh start on the problem without being unduly influenced by preconceived notions or by being told

what is "impossible." Many people have become famous by doing the "impossible," such as designing a horseless carriage or a flying machine.

To develop new methods and obtain the "impossible," try general orders. Make them specific only as far as purpose and objectives are concerned. Point out the pitfalls encountered by others in working on the same problem. But don't place too low a ceiling on a man by being overly explicit on details. And don't be surprised if the "impossible" is occasionally accomplished.

For Strict Accountability

Oral orders suffice for most cases but, when you want to hold someone strictly accountable, follow the motto "put it in writing." When clearly expressed, the written word cannot be disputed and will be available for reference, whereas a spoken order may be forgotten or its meaning lost as days go by.

When the sequence of an operation is highly important, written directions enable a man to do the job step by step in the exact manner desired. Writing also beats speaking when precise figures or complicated details are involved. This doesn't necessarily mean that you need to have a typed letter of instructions. A penciled order can provide an effective, lasting record.

To Get a Disagreeable Job Done

Some jobs are "above and beyond the call of ordinary duty." They may be disagreeable or require painstaking care or exceptional attention to detail. Perhaps they are somewhat dangerous or call for overtime at inconvenient hours. When such work is assigned directly, the "unlucky" person may feel that he has been singled out as the "goat" in an unfair manner. His fellow workers will probably agree with him and sympathize. When a call is made for volunteers on annoying tasks, however, the response is often surprising. The job may prove a challenge that gives someone an opportunity to demonstrate his ability, to obtain added recognition, or to secure the self-satisfaction which comes with the completion of an intricate task. However, the supervisor should not use the volunteer method to escape the responsibility for making assignments that are fair to all workers in the group and practical for production.

To Reduce Your Worries

If it's necessary to use untrained or inexperienced people, the supervisor may have plenty of reason to worry about accuracy and meeting schedules, and he should worry if he has been vague or overly brief in his instructions. Detailed orders, oral or written, are needed to keep the man with limited experience "on the beam." Although detailed instructions are annoying for simple assignments or for a trained person, they are a must for those who are untrained. Detailed orders also reduce your worries about infrequent or special jobs (where the worker's unfamiliarity with the job may cause trouble) or in cases where the procedure has been changed. They are also valuable for instructional purposes.

To Instruct

The principles of good instruction involve four steps, as many supervisors will remember from job instruction training conferences. First, prepare the worker. Second, tell and show the procedure, stressing "key points." Third, have him do the job. Fourth, put him on his own, and check results. For further

details on proper job instruction, refer to the J.I.T. card and manual prepared by the War Manpower Commission.

Be a Leader, Not a "Boss"

Since orders are the connecting link between you and the team, they determine whether you are a real leader or a driver. People yearn for effective leadership. They do not like the strain of working without wise direction. On the other hand, they want to see some of their own ideas respected and used. They will not cooperate to the fullest extent with the boss who dominates the scene, orders them around like children, or fails to integrate the work of everyone into real accomplishment. Tailor your orders and the manner in which they are delivered to suit both the individual and the situation. Be sure they will get the job done correctly, quickly, conscientiously. When orders are *thoroughly understood and carried out*, you have done a good job as a supervisor.

8

Do the Best with What You Have

THE supervisor's job is relatively easy when he is assigned a team that is highly trained and has a background of wide experience. Many a supervisor, however, does not find himself in such an ideal situation. It is often necessary to use employees in positions which may be above their present abilities

and which, therefore, furnish a real challenge both to the workers and to the supervisors who must train and direct them.

Supervisors' reactions to this situation vary greatly with individual experience, ingenuity, and sense of responsibility. Some gripe about the matter and blame low quality and quantity on their teams. Others consider the situation to be hopeless and philosophically refuse even to gripe about it. Still others, though realizing their handicaps, *do the best with what they have*, realizing it is their job to use everyone to the best of his ability and to uncover and develop hidden or dormant talent.

If you are not hopelessly without hope, you may have summed up your problem something like this, "How can I get the best possible production out of each person?"

Use Outstanding Qualities

In attacking this problem, first of all determine the one or two outstanding qualities or abilities of each team member. Analyze both those who are obviously good and those who are

REALLY KNOW EACH MAN OR WOMAN

at first glance inferior. Be sure that you really know each man or woman well enough so that you are not overlooking some undeveloped talent. Then, knowing what ability is dominant, *use it to the utmost* by practical training, helpful coaching, intelligent instruction, and timely encouragement. Have no fear that a worker will fail if you really use him to the best of his ability. On the other hand, you may be quite sure that his performance will be only what he thinks you expect of him.

Often a young or inexperienced worker is hampered as much by lack of confidence as by lack of training. If such is the case, be doubly sure that he knows when he has done a satisfactory job. Then, as he gains confidence in his ability along one line, it will be easier to encourage him to develop along other lines. "Nothing succeeds like success," and when a worker successfully completes one assignment, he has more faith in his ability to do the next job, even if it requires greater effort.

But don't expect men and women to gain confidence or succeed through success merely because you pat them on the back. The first consideration must be selection of proper assignments for your team members. Rather than make a snap judgment as to whether a man or woman can do certain jobs on your team, look over desirable combinations of assignments and persons. Remember that a few outstanding characteristics may make or break a person in a given type of job. Work in industry is highly versatile, and there is a variety of assignments that can be handled efficiently by people with widely different abilities. Some of the abilities vitally needed are the following:

1. Ability to secure information (An inquiring attitude may often serve a good purpose even though technical knowledge is below par)
2. Leadership ability that is needed in an assistant supervisor or understudy (Develop the person who shows he is a natural leader)
3. Planning and organizing ability (Maybe the employee who cocks an eyebrow at some of your ideas could help a lot on planning and administration)
4. Ability to check the work of others because of an innate desire for accuracy (The obstinate chap who would "rather be right than president" might help eliminate errors)
5. Ability to do original creative work (The "idea man" is going to sprout ideas anyhow; why not tie him down and use his best ones?)
6. Knowledge and experience in the work of other departments (Don't hold it against a man because he sees the

viewpoint of another department; his ideas may save time and money)

THE "IDEA MAN" WHY NOT USE HIM?

Know your employees well enough so that you can quickly and accurately gauge their talents along all these lines. Perhaps someone who is doing a good routine job also has an unusual knack for unearthing information, and you can increase his usefulness and make him happier if you see that he has plenty of this type of work to do. Another may exhibit a potential ability to do the highest type jobs in your group. In this case, it will pay you well to give him every opportunity to increase his usefulness by assigning jobs of a progressively more important nature rather than to hold him down to prosaic work. In some cases, it may not be possible to use a person in the highest grade of work he can do, but whenever possible an employee should be used to the best of his ability.

Work on the Weak Points

The good qualities of an employee may sometimes be uncovered only by a diligent search, while his weak points are usually more obvious and may sometimes be driven home with great force when an unsatisfactory job results. However, it is as dangerous to assume that a man has no weaknesses because he does a generally satisfactory job as to assume that he has no value because his weaknesses are more apparent.

It is well to know the most pronounced weaknesses of each employee so that these may be corrected by proper training or at least counterbalanced by other personnel. Be sure that each employee is aware of his shortcomings and has also been told what to do about them. To correct weaknesses, best results come from concentrating on one or two specific points at a time, especially those where the greatest improvement can result.

Typical weaknesses of employees are the following:

Lack of familiarity with the company's products (Have they been given opportunities to learn?)

Inaccuracy (Have you coached them thoroughly in correction of the errors they have made?)

LACKADAISICAL ATTITUDE

Lack of familiarity with standard procedures (Do they see these things as helpful, logical aids to consistent production or as an unintelligible maze of rules?)

Lackadaisical attitude (Is it due to lack of interest, lack of training, improper assignments, or preoccupation with personal problems?)

These and other weaknesses in employees are aggravated by rapid company expansion and the resulting necessity for using people with limited training. Personnel men cannot wave a magic wand and secure dozens of applicants with the exact experience required. Some of those who are hired must of necessity be recent high-school or college graduates or people recruited from other companies and industries.

Your problem is to develop men and women quickly so that 100 per cent of their time can be spent on productive work—work that they can do well because it matches their aptitude and training. It is also your problem to see that they prepare themselves to fill jobs of higher responsibility. If you can do this, it is one of the best indications of your ability as a supervisor.

9

The New Employee

Do you recall your first day on your first full-time job?

No matter how confident you were when you were graduated from school, the chances are you lost a good deal of it as you walked into your new workplace for the first time. Perhaps it did you good to lose some of your overconfidence, but not to replace it with doubts, uncertainties, and fears.

THEY'RE NOT FAR DIFFERENT

All new employees have doubts as to their ability to make good and feel somewhat ill at ease in the midst of strange faces and strange surroundings and when confronted with unfamiliar situations. They may stick their chins out and walk with a determined stride, but they're not far different from the small boy whistling as he walks by a cemetery late at night.

To ensure rapid adjustment to productive work, new employees need to be put at ease, made to feel at home, given confidence in their new company and their group, furnished information on local rules and customs, and provided with the proper point of view *right at the start.* Special attention must be given their first assignments, which should be as interesting as possible and helpful in getting them oriented to their new situation.

A new employee is probably not assigned to your group every day or week or even every month. But any day you do have a new member on your team, the matter of introducing him to his job is as important as any problem you have that day. The impressions a new employee obtains during the first day are impressions that stay with him a long time. By making every effort to introduce him properly to his job in the beginning, you can save yourself time and trouble later on, since no one works at his best when he is uninformed or misinformed or made to feel that he is no more important than a piece of equipment.

Three Case Histories

That proper orientation is necessary for new employees is demonstrated by three actual cases in which someone slipped up in introducing a new employee to his job.

Case I. One employee, well paid for his job, complained to the personnel department that he couldn't possibly live on the wages he was receiving and that both he and his wife were dissatisfied. Further conversation revealed that they were living in a small room, ate all their meals in restaurants, and hence had little opportunity for a happy home life. For some reason, the man did not know that suitable apartments or houses were available, but the couple was referred to a home where they could do their own cooking and live the usual lives of domestic-minded people.

Case II. Another new employee was practically ignored for two entire weeks and was on the point of leaving his new job. The reason for his plight was that the group head was busy taking a conference in job-relations training, and the assistant head was working on a rush job. When finally given an interesting assignment that called for some hard work, this employee did a creditable job.

Case III. One woman worked for a few months and later entered a company training school when a new class was started. Asked how she liked school compared with actual work, she sincerely stated, "It's much tougher at school. You've got to get your work in on time. They don't ignore you."

These are three actual cases, none of which is typical, we hope, but which illustrate the importance of proper induction procedure by both the personnel representative and the supervisor.

In order to save time for supervisors, personnel departments are paying special attention to welcoming the new employee and furnishing him with the information he needs to have. This good work can be nullified if the supervisor fails to take over where personnel leaves off. However, there should be no unnecessary duplication between the efforts of personnel representatives and the supervisor in doing this orientation work. The following is an outline of a successful plan for dividing the orientation procedure, as used in the engineering department of The Glenn L. Martin Company.

What Does Personnel Do?

Once the selection of an employee has been made, on the basis of interviews, experience, and education records, employee induction procedure is as follows:

1. He signs the necessary papers, undergoes a physical examination, and is photographed and fingerprinted in the personnel department.
2. He reports for an induction interview with a personnel representative and has a chance to ask specific questions

about his new job and employment conditions. He is given information on company history, products, rules, and regulations; personnel services (housing, transportation, insurance, pensions, banking, etc.); pertinent facts about pay, merit ratings, wage increases, educational opportunities, etc.
3. He is made acquainted, in a general way, with the organization and taken on an inspection tour of the shops.
4. He is introduced to his immediate supervisor by a personnel representative.

5. Special attention is given to see that he is trained for his job, perhaps in a training school, either full or part time. At any rate, a personal tailor-made program for advancement is outlined.
6. A follow-up interview is arranged with each new employee about a month after appointment to determine if he is properly placed and well established in the job, the company, and the community. The progress and adjustment of the new employee are continually checked by personnel counselors, who assist all employees with personal and business problems, and educational counselors, who recommend courses and reading for immediate job requirements or advancement.

This procedure is helpful in adjusting people to new conditions, which may be far different from those to which they have been accustomed. But it is also important that the supervisor devote special attention to the orientation of each new employee.

What Should the Supervisor Do?

Your first job in meeting the new employee is to make him feel at home and glad that he is a part of the group to which he has been assigned. This should be foremost in your mind the first day and the first week. Welcome the new employee in a friendly manner and put him at ease by discussing something of mutual interest. Introduce him to his fellow employees as soon as possible. Take him to your own boss and be sure that he meets at least one or two of the top supervisors or executives at some convenient time.

You or your boss should explain the specific functions of the group in detail, following up the general explanation by the personnel department. Outline the new employee's specific duties and responsibilities and show him that his work is needed, even though it comprises but a small portion of the total effort. Encourage his questions and answer them sincerely with no attempt at overselling or underselling.

The new employee will be deeply interested in his workplace and the facilities available to the group. He will need to know where to go for supplies and for information.

A few questions will indicate whether or not he is well housed and provided with a satisfactory ride to work. If there are any unsolved problems, take him back to the personnel department for further assistance.

Remember that a mass of information is given the new person in his first day or two on the job and, though he is furnished with printed information, he will still have unanswered questions. You may not have time to do all the question answering and orientation yourself, but some sympathetic member of your group can be entrusted with a portion of the job. Keep in mind that the orientation procedure is an assignment that only you or your best subordinate is qualified to handle. It is not a job for a clerk under any circumstances.

There are some things that should definitely be done the first day by you or a member of your group whom you have trained for the job. The following will serve as a check list:

1. By all means, have lunch with the new employee as evidence of your interest, as well as to acquaint him with restaurant facilities.

EXPLAIN THE TIME CLOCK

2. Take him to his time clock, if one is used, and explain the proper procedure for punching in and out, including starting and quitting time.

3. Show the location of the rest room, files, and other points of interest.
4. Discuss routine daily procedures, explaining fully "how" and "why."

Many supervisors have established the practice of seeing each new employee at the end of the first working day to be certain he feels at home and will come back the next day "rarin' to go."

At convenient times during the first week or so, it is well to assure yourself that matters such as vacations and group insurance have been explained fully. Since we all are apt to mistrust those things which we don't understand, it is essential that a clear picture be obtained by the employee of all the rules, regulations, and services.

Whether he asks it or not, the employee will be keenly interested in wage raises and possibilities for promotion. In these matters, it is not wise to make promises, since the progress of the employee depends on his future performance, which cannot always be predicted accurately. You can, and should, point out the possible paths of promotion and perhaps mention the progress of typical employees. It should be made plain, however, that promotions depend on quality and quantity of work, attitudes, and the extent to which he trains himself in preparation for higher work.

The First Assignment

The surest way to get a person off to the right start is to provide him with work assignments that whet his interest and get him into worth-while production. Don't just give him something to fill up his time. You may be tempted to say, "Here's the company reference manual. Read it." However, the usual reference manual is not suitable for such instructional purposes.

Before starting the new man on the job, you will have reviewed his education and experience record and become generally familiar with what he has done and can do. These data and further questioning will reveal his qualifications and limitations and enable you to assign his first job intelligently. You will, no doubt, have planned some specific work that will be useful in this orientation. Requirements of desirable first assignments are as follows:

1. Suited to the worker—not too elementary or routine, not too complicated
2. As interesting as possible
3. Educational (Give him an opportunity to use equipment, information sources, etc., which he will be using in his later work)
4. Worth while; that is, actual production jobs, not work that won't be used

HIS WORK BEING PUT TO USE--

All the rules of good instruction and good supervision that apply to any worker apply also to the new member of your team—only more so. Take special precautions to make assignments complete and understandable.

Some supervisors build up a high degree of enthusiasm by showing the new employee how his work is later put to use. The average draftsman, for example, gets a lift from seeing a part he has drawn being actually produced in the shop.

Close Checkup

The new employee naturally requires closer attention than one who has established himself. It is necessary to gain his confidence and respect. Show that you trust him, and he'll try harder to merit your trust. Criticism of his first work should be kindly, sympathetic, and constructive, but nevertheless firm. Although emphasis on quantity will come a little later, accuracy needs to be stressed from the very beginning. Remember the stimulating effects of sincere praise as soon as he gives you reason to bestow it.

You have done a good job in orienting the new employee if he

Feels that he's a part of the group.

Realizes his importance to the team.

Has confidence in you, the team, the department, the company, and the product.

Understands the company rules and policies that he needs to know and the reasons behind them.

Knows where to secure information.

Realizes the importance of good work and proper attitude as a basis for promotion.

Has a desire to fit himself for higher rated work.

And above all, if he has been placed in work suited to his abilities so he is producing what is expected.

Have your attitude and actions won his friendship? his respect? his confidence?

10

How to Lose Workers and Alienate Bosses

THERE are certain sure-fire methods by which a supervisor can annoy his workers, alienate his bosses, and make people dislike him vigorously.

These methods are based on various *attitudes* (and resultant actions), which are either inherent or have been developed.

Investigation reveals that the following types of supervisors are most effective in disrupting morale, killing enthusiasm, and lowering quality and quantity of production:

The "Staller"
The "So-whatter"
The "Noncooperator"
The "Quack"
"Old Unreliable"
The "Gestapo Agent"
The "Grandstander"
The "Represser"
The "Surpriser"

It is not necessary to be a combination of these types in order to irritate and annoy. An aptitude in any one of these classes can send you speedily on the road to unpopularity.

It is not even necessary actually to be one of these types. Give people the *impression* that you are a "Grandstander" or "Gestapo Agent" or "Old Unreliable." It has the same effect.

For further study and analysis of these types in action, we present the supervisory Rogue's Gallery.

The "Staller"

"Never do today what tomorrow you can put off until another day." That is the motto of the hesitating, stalling, evasive supervisor. The stalling technique is unfailing in its ability to irritate progressive people. It can disrupt not only your own group but dozens of others that are dependent on your decisions and the completion of your work.

THE TIMID "STALLER"

"Stallers" are of two types: (1) timid "Stallers" and (2) shouting "Stallers." The timid type appears bashful and spineless and acts as if he were afraid to make up his mind. However, he is not so dangerous as the shouting "Staller," who appears decisive but is really just the opposite. He is the man who roars out a decision one day, only to reverse it the next. His roaring and loud language are an attempt to cover ignorance or laziness or lack of backbone. Psychologists would say he has a "superiority complex."[1]

If you want to enhance your reputation as a Staller simply fail to study a problem; neglect to get all the facts; becloud the main issues. Then, it will be impossible for you to make a prompt, clear-cut decision. You will have hit the heights of hesitation.

The "So-whatter"

The "So-whatter" is easy to imitate. He has a standard comeback for any disagreeable situation. The work is a week behind time. So what? Someone made a mistake. So what?

"So-whatters" are made, not born. Practice over a period

[1] A superiority complex is defined as a form of inferiority complex whereby a person attempts to conceal and compensate for his inferiority by a superior manner (boasting, loud talk, swaggering, etc.).

of years is necessary in order to achieve the professional bored, cynical outlook of the *true* "So-whatter"

This indifferent type has several irritation techniques. He ignores the suggestions made by his workers. He makes no attempt to understand and put into effect the directives of his superior. He looks down his nose at efficiency, schedules, company rules. He just says, "So what."

The "Noncooperator"

Related to the "So-whatter," but with distinct characteristics of his own, is the "Noncooperator." It's not his mode of operation to work in harmony with his men, his superiors, or other groups.

He shuts himself out from the ideas, desires, and preferences of other people. He doesn't recognize the organizational setup of his department and company. He is secretive about his own ideas and methods, and hoards information that may aid others.

The "Noncooperator" never goes out of his way to help anyone. He doesn't seek the advice or consent of his workers, is not interested in becoming well informed on management techniques, and feels that he has no responsibility in training his team in their jobs.

Forget your associates completely if you want to be known as a "Noncooperator."

The "Quack"

The "Quack" is recognized by his pseudo-clever, insincere attitude. He hands out a cheery greeting, slaps you on the back,

THE "QUACK"

and praises you to the skies. But his interest is only skin deep. He alternately pampers and threatens, flatters and bullies.

Call yourself "Napoleon." Devise grand strategies for getting what you want. Put on a front. Pretend to be something you aren't. Blame the others for all the mistakes that are made. These are time-tested ways in which you can become a "Quack."

"Old Unreliable"

The "Unreliable" type can always be depended on—to break promises, to get behind schedule, or to encourage inferior work. He will promise to have a job done this week; it's a miracle if it's ever completed. Those who aspire to be highly unreliable should neglect planning, assign jobs indiscriminately, tackle unimportant tasks first.

You can't help being annoying, irritating, and unpopular if you follow two rules: (1) make plenty of promises; (2) break them all.

The "Gestapo Agent"

"Gestapo" methods are not confined to dictator-dominated nations. You can be a "Gestapo Agent" in your own office.

THE "GESTAPO AGENT"

Distrust your workers. Continually act as if you are spying on your men, as if you expected them to do something disastrous. Be extremely suspicious of other groups, always expecting a stab in the back. Gestapo motto: Do others before they do you.

The "Grandstander"

The "Grandstander" loves to run with the ball and make a touchdown. It's *the team's job* when the thinking is to be done. And it's *his job* to take the glory. A simple rule for the "Grandstander" is to take credit for everything except failure. Never admit that one of your men is doing a fine job. Neglect to give credit where credit is due. It won't take the team long to recognize you as a man who likes to be in the limelight, taking undeserved bows. This will irritate your superior, but its greatest

THE "GRANDSTANDER"

effect will be to deflate the enthusiasm of your workers. They'll make you No. 1 on their Hiss Parade.

The "Represser"

To be a clever Machiavellian "Represser," hold your subordinates down to your own level. Stifle every hint of original thinking. Stymie every progressive action. The degree of your unpopularity will depend on your ability to repress, suppress, depress.

The "Surpriser"

The "Surpriser" has a marvelous twofold opportunity for disgusting his men and obtaining devilish glee for himself. It's not for him to let people know in advance about changes that affect them. To be a "Surpriser," spring something new at the most critical moment. Wait until all your workers are functioning at top-notch efficiency under present plans; then march right in and upset everything. Don't worry too much about whether or not the change is desirable. The element of surprise will prevent organized opposition. Do all these things, and you can't fail to annoy.

NOTE: Any resemblance between these characters and any industrial supervisors is purely coincidental.

11

Good Business Manners

With no desire to turn business organizations into "pink teas" . . .

Caring not a rap about "society" as such . . .

With disregard for *silly* rules and stuffiness . . .

And with no ambition to replace Emily Post, author of *Etiquette* (the bluebook of social usage) . . .

But definitely believing that efficiency and good human relations can be improved by more consideration of other peoples' interests and feelings, we present suggestions on *Good Business Manners* (the bluebook of business usage).

Just how important are good manners in the business world?

Says Emily Post, "No one—unless he be a recluse who comes in contact with no other human being—can fail to reap the advantage of a courteous and likable approach, or fail to be handicapped by an improper, offensive, and resented one."

According to an engineer, "A courteous, cooperative, and unprejudiced attitude in dealing with others is the foundation of good business manners. Remember, the other fellow has a job to do and that job is important. Whether he is able to produce or not may depend on your ability and, more significantly, on your willingness to assist. Although individuals may be identified by departments, it should be realized that all these departments add up to make a team, not a contest. Don't ignore others simply because they work in another department or because their jobs are not as big as you think yours is. Good business manners do not permit intolerable attitudes based on jealousy or superiority."

If you are considerate of other people when you ask for their cooperation; if you maintain a helpful attitude when others come to you; if you know how to take orders and how to give them; if you avoid irritating attitudes and mannerisms, and if you treat people as individuals, then—and only then—do you possess good business manners.

DON'T IGNORE OTHERS---

The following suggestions come from executives, supervisors, and a wide range of employees who were asked what constitutes good business manners today.

When Seeing Others

If the people who make unnecessary business calls were laid end to end, many a company would look like a dormitory. To keep from being a social lion, who makes people want to duck out when he appears, be sure that your business visits are necessary. Executives appreciate a person who has something vital to say, says it, and knows when to leave. Stalling around to impress the boss with your conversation and presence may boomerang. What many people forget, however, is that fellow employees, as well as bosses, merit this same consideration of their time.

A pest of the first order is he who interrupts a discussion with the too familiar phrase "This won't take long." No matter how important a subject is to you, it may seem trivial to someone else. If the person you want to see is busy, come back later or, if absolutely necessary, wait patiently for a sign of recognition and a statement of when your turn will come. Often a quick phone call for an appointment will save time and energy and get your problem more concentrated attention.

But don't conserve your energy to the extent of yelling across the room rather than walking over to another desk and confining your interruptions to one person. Loud conversations disturb everyone in the vicinity. The well-mannered worker is inconspicuous and unobtrusive and realizes that efficient discussions take place at close range.

When Others Call on You

A "big" person is often easier to see than a "little" one because he realizes the importance of giving a visitor courtesy and attention in return for the time and trouble taken to seek him

PLACE A CALLER AT EASE

out. He knows that poor business manners suggest incompetence. Only the small fry, with an exaggerated sense of importance, gives others the cold shoulder.

Acknowledge immediately a person who comes to see you. If temporarily busy on a hot job, excuse yourself and arrange to see the caller later. Place a caller at ease by being at ease yourself and displaying a friendly, sincere interest. Keep in mind that in any conversation the most popular person is the listener. Listen tolerantly and considerately with an open mind, giving the visitor your undivided attention. Try to see the other fellow's viewpoint and, if you can be of assistance to him, throw your heart and soul into it. Don't feel that in giving help you are doing a favor. Chances are, you are being paid for it. Furthermore, it is seldom that the "instructor" fails to learn something of value himself.

There will be times when you'll feel like telling a visitor to scram because his business is over. However, anyone can develop subtle suggestive methods for obtaining the same result courteously.

Receiving Orders

It's an Army axiom that no one is qualified to give orders until he knows how to take them. In getting an assignment, be "all ears." Ask any questions needed to clarify your boss's instructions. The final result should be a true meeting of minds and, when that has occurred, it is time to leave. Repress the urge to describe in detail how you will handle the job, unless he asks you. He is interested in the results you bring back. An indication that you "will attend to the matter" notifies your supervisor that you understand the job.

Giving Orders

Orders aren't barked out any more, except in the movies and by old-fashioned supervisors who haven't learned efficient techniques. Mix proper amounts of friendliness and firmness to secure the cooperation you want.

Although orders must be brief and easy to follow, they also need to be detailed enough to give a clear picture. They are not courteous unless they are complete. Test their completeness by means of these six short questions. Have you told Who? What? Why? When? Where? How?

Women in Industry

Women workers are almost unanimous in saying they want to be treated in the same way as men. Both the men and the women agree that sex has no place in the business world unless you are running a night club. Women are hired in industry today because they are needed to do important work. In some cases they are in jobs to which they are accustomed; in others, they are in jobs that formerly were filled only by men. It is up to a supervisor to respect them for their abilities, to instruct them whenever needed, to encourage efficient work, and to refrain from being too friendly. Women should be called Miss or Mrs.—

or at least by their first names—never "Hey, Babe." Offensive nicknames and vulgarity are resented. A safe rule for a supervisor to follow is to treat women workers the same way he would desire his sister or wife to be treated if working.

On the Telephone

When the television principle is perfected, telephone manners will probably be vastly improved. But even now, when you aren't able to see the other person, you can display courtesy by promptness in answering, by clear and natural speech, by brevity, and in many other ways.

Do you follow these rules for courteous, efficient telephone messages, recommended by telephone companies?

1. Answer promptly to keep from irritating the person calling you.
2. For efficiency, give your group name and your own name. The "Hello" answer is out of date.
3. Speak clearly and distinctly in a natural tone of voice that's easy to understand. Avoid whispering, shouting, mumbling.

4. Handle the call yourself, if you can, rather than transferring it to someone else. It's a nuisance to have to go over the same ground two or even three times. But if you don't know the answer, turn it over to someone who does, rather than discuss the matter at length, then wind up by saying, "You'll have to talk to someone else."
5. Signal the operator for transferring a call to another phone by moving the receiver hook up and down slowly three times, then pause; repeat if necessary.
6. Make notes of phone conversations, particularly if you are taking a message for another person. Keep a pad and pencil handy, so you won't have to hunt for them.
7. If you plan to be away, let someone else know where you'll be, in case you're wanted by telephone.

LET SOMEONE KNOW WHERE YOU'LL BE

8. Listen attentively so repetitions won't be necessary. Don't interrupt, argue, or become impatient.
9. When a secretary asks your name before connecting you with her boss, don't take it as a personal affront or accuse her of being officious. She is carrying out orders, and if you have been around a bit you will accept it as a matter of course.
10. When you have received the information you want, it does no harm to say, "Thank you"—don't just hang up and leave the other person dangling on the line. (Secretaries say this applies particularly to people who, when told the person they're calling is out, answer with a click of the receiver.)

11. After saying, "Goodbye," replace the receiver gently. Don't give the other person a "crack in the ear."

Irritations

A group of employees was asked what violations of good business manners were their pet peeves. These were the results:

"People who interrupt you in the middle of a sentence"

"Blustering and bluffing"

OVER-EFFUSIVE GREETINGS

"Nasty personal habits, such as picking nose, dirty nails"

"Lack of ability to overlook lack of manners in others"

"Unwillingness to do a simple favor"

"Men's prejudiced attitudes against women workers"

"Obvious lack of interest"

"Failure to greet subordinates in corridors"

"People who interrupt private discussions"

"Walking into an office, either as if you owned it or as if you wouldn't own it if given to you"

"Favoritism in manners toward certain individuals"

"Overeffusive hand shakes or salutations"

"The man who is too proud to say, 'Thank you'"

Personality

A likable personality (the sum total of your characteristics) is a definite business asset. "Personality," says Emily Post, "can be cultivated sometimes, but only by something added to skill or character or knowledge, and never by assumed tricks of manner."

As one step in improving your personality, submerge your own selfish interests. Help others to do a good job without seeking credit. Work for the good of the team.

12

Being Fair to the Fairer Sex

or

"Some Serious Words on How to Cope with Women in Industry and Maintain Maximum Production"
(Written by a woman[1] from a woman's standpoint)

SPEAKING of women—and men frequently do—let's first cast out this attitude of the Arabs-stole-silently-in-while-we-were-off-guard-and-have-pitched-their-tents. The feeling that women have invaded an industrial realm created especially for masculine occupancy will start us off on the wrong foot. Not trespassers these women—but invited participants.

Starting with this point of view (and the added fact that they are here, for better or for worse, until industry doth cease), let's examine a few suggestions the supervisor can use to obtain maximum efficiency, morale, and production from the feminine members of his group.

Give Her the Benefit of the Doubt

Imagine yourself—an engineer, office manager, or shop foreman—through some quirk of fate working in a dressmaking establishment. Would you feel at home? How productive would you be at first? How much assistance would you expect from your supervisor?

Remember, the success of a new female worker is largely dependent upon the start you give her. The supervisor who scans a new girl with a jaundiced eye and thinks almost out loud,

[1] Doris M. Schaefer, Engineering Personnel Department, The Glenn L. Martin Company.

"Humph! Vogue exterior, vague interior!" is licked from the start. And if his team is not functioning up to his expectation, it might well be that the fault lies with the supervisor rather than with his workers.

Intolerance is one of the symptoms of intellectual deficiency. So, before you accuse her of being under par, greet the new employee with an open mind and *give her a chance.* You may reap the benefits.

THE ENGINEER AS A DRESSMAKER

Your women workers, even after they have become familiar with their own particular jobs, do not instinctively see themselves and their jobs in relation to the over-all picture of production, as do men who are accustomed to industrial organizations. It is important to give women an intelligible picture of other departments, the interdependence of departments, and the importance of the job they are doing as a part of the completed product.

Answer Her Questions

One of the best indications of interest in the job is the development of a questioning attitude, and women are notably inquisitive. Experts agree that this is a sure sign that the brain cells are alive. Discouragement of this trait will do more to lower morale than almost any other thing you could do. Don't be too busy to give the beginner a considered answer, even though the question seems elementary or irrelevant.

In a survey[1] conducted by a national magazine, it was reported that 82 per cent of the participants felt that women like to have their work reviewed more frequently than do men. Often they have more personal pride in what they are doing than men, and frequent attention will bring about best performance on the job.

Women Are Individuals

Beware of putting all women members of your department in the same category. Women are just as much individuals as men. The wise supervisor studies his workers' individual capabilities and concentrates on their development. Ask yourself, "Is

WOMEN ARE INDIVIDUALS

this woman slow or quick to learn? Is she adaptable to routine work? Does her maximum efficiency depend on interest, appreciation, or attention?" All these individual traits must be recognized and utilized to secure her best efforts. Go over her merit rating with her. It will help you spot individual characteristics and make a fairer evaluation, not only of her performance, but of her capacity as well.

[1] Schultz, Richard S., "Are Women Workers Cooperative?" *Supervision*, February, 1943, p. 28.

Treat Her on an Equal Basis with Men

Women taking over men's jobs and responsibilities almost unanimously prefer to be treated in the same way as the men working beside them. In most cases they neither demand nor want special attention. Flattery to them is a mark of insincerity. Favoritism indicates that intelligence and efficiency on the job are not being recognized.

FLATTERY TO THEM IS A MARK OF INSINCERITY

Nothing so quenches the spark of enthusiasm as being ignored when information is passed out, a practice that makes a woman feel she is not an integral part of the team. On the other hand, nothing is more conducive to a serious, interested approach to work than the feeling of being considered a valuable member of the team who must be kept up to scratch on last-minute items.

Don't Make Her Feel Insignificant

One of the most frequent complaints voiced by women employees is that men are antagonistic toward them. Perhaps the factor that contributes most to this feeling is the attitude on the part of men that their feminine coworkers are just filling in temporarily. This may or may not be true. However, we have learned that "temporarily" may mean a long, long time. A good supervisor can develop latent abilities to advantage if he gives his women workers the same attention he gives the men in his department. In short, don't make your girls feel like asking, "Where does an alien go to register?"

Keep in mind that all workers like to know that their abilities will be recognized and that their opportunities for advancement will be entirely dependent upon a combination of these abilities with effort, enthusiasm, and interest. Assign them jobs they believe they can handle. Who knows? Perhaps they recognize their capabilities and limitations better than you realize. And after all, willingness to try a job is an important factor—the first step toward successful completion of a job by any employee, man or woman.

Consider Feminine Characteristics

Actually, this problem of supervision of "coeds," boiled down, is similar to that for men if you consider the characteristics that are present in both men and women, but perhaps more obvious or pronounced among the latter.

WOMEN ARE MORE SENSITIVE TO THEIR ENVIRONMENT —

The consensus among psychologists, film directors, business magnates, and savants of the social world (and where could one find a more representative estimate?) is that successful handling of the fairer sex depends upon a knowledge of feminine differences. To be brief, it is important to bear in mind the following when faced with the problem of keeping your coeds in line:

Women are a little more sociable on the job than men. Occasionally it is necessary to bring them down to business in this respect.

Women are more sensitive to criticism and praise than men. Absence of criticism is not the equivalent of praise. Give them straightforward, constructive, detailed criticism. But in the same spirit of trying to get the job done quickly and correctly, measure out deserved praise with equally constructive and detailed consideration.

Women are more sensitive to their environment. Consider how you can provide the most comfortable working conditions. Women are responsible for many improved conditions now enjoyed by both men and women.

Women's physical differences should be considered. Heavy lifting and work involving superendurance should not be expected of them. The workplace, tables, files, etc., should be arranged to suit their height.

13

Timeconomy and Job Planning

Does work pile up on your desk?

Do job worries make your life miserable?

Are you always behind time?

If so, the answer to your woes may be planning.

Today's politicians and writers have somewhat overworked the words "plan" and "planning," what with war plans, peace

DOES WORK PILE UP?

plans, 5-year plans, etc. Despite the way "plans" have been kicked around and made needlessly complicated, there is plenty of place in industry for simple logical *thinking ahead.*

What Is Planning?

According to Webster, a plan is a "method or scheme of action, procedure, or arrangement; project, program, outline, or schedule."

An authority on supervision[1] calls planning "outlining and setting up a system that expects the unexpected and can take care of it when it arrives."

Planning requires a well-defined objective; it involves budgeting time; it substitutes thinking for worry; it means looking ahead to tomorrow, next week, next month, next year; it provides for "ifs," "ands," and "buts."

For the average supervisor, proper planning means work finished on time, more effective use of man power, improved morale, better quality of work. It will pay him well to plan (1) his personal working time and (2) each job assigned to his group.

TIMECONOMY

About 30 per cent of the total time in your entire week is officially designated as your work week. That doesn't include

[1] Walton, Albert, *Do You Want to Be a Foreman?* McGraw-Hill Book Company, Inc., New York, 1941.

the time you spend worrying after hours, nor is waste time deducted.

No matter whether you are the most efficient supervisor ever, or a novice, you have *time* in equal quantity. How you spend that time determines your worth as a supervisor.

There are two important considerations in evaluating your working time:

1. Do you distribute it wisely?
2. Do you spend it efficiently?

Spread Your Time Wisely

If you spend too much time on correspondence, details, and routine work, you will not have the time and energy that should be allotted to supervision of your group and helpful conferences with your superiors and other groups.

Examples of Time Budgets[1]

Duty	*Technical supervisors*	*Nontechnical supervisors*	*Executives*	*Staff consultants*	*You*	
					Actual	*Desirable*
Planning (scheduling jobs; outlining work procedure; thinking ahead)	7	12	7	11		
Production or creative work (personal work not assigned to your men)	12	0	4	12		
Correspondence and report writing	1	2	4	4		
Conferences with subordinates (assignments, instruction, job follow-up)	15	22	7	3		
Conferences with superiors	6	6	4	3		
Conferences with other groups (securing or giving information; cooperative work)	7	6	16	11		
Contacts outside company	0	0	6	4		
Total	48	48	48	48		

[1] Engineering Department, The Glenn L. Martin Company.

In order to allot your vital man-hours wisely, a *time budget* may prove helpful. The time budgets in the accompanying chart show the wide variations in distribution of time by supervisors, executives, and staff consultants. The figures given are averages of typical persons in each classification. Note that supervisors spend a great deal of time in conferences with subordinates; executives distribute their time more evenly over a large number of activities; staff consultants are heavy on planning, personal creative work, conferences with other groups.

NO NEED FOR A STOP WATCH...

Your personal time budget need not be a complicated system that annoys you or takes valuable time in operating. Simply write down in the right-hand column of the accompanying chart the amount of time you owe to each function. It will only take a few minutes to prepare this preliminary time budget.

Choose a typical week in which to check the time you actually spend on different types of activities. You don't have to hold a stop watch on yourself. Just jot down your time distribution at the end of each day. When Saturday comes, the totals may prove to be a surprise.

It may be that you will want to revise your time budget slightly to make it more practical. However, don't allow one or two items to steal the show and result in neglect of other equally important duties. Be sure none of your responsibilities suffers from lack of time and attention.

No two men need have exactly the same time budget. It all depends on the nature of your work and your individual ability.

Spend Your Time Efficiently

A 48-hour work week consists of 2,880 minutes, and a 40-hour week consists of 2,400 minutes. Take care of these minutes, and the hours will take care of themselves. Here are a few time-saving tips that may help you increase your work output.

Planning

Most supervisors will find it inadvisable to cut down on planning time. For planning is a way in which time can be conserved in every other supervisory function. Planning involves a consideration of things that will needlessly consume time and the taking of steps to prevent interruptions and delays.

Long-range planning is essential, but so is day-to-day planning. One device that can help you perform your duties in an orderly fashion at the proper time is a *tickler file.* Here's how to start one: Prepare a set of 31 manila folders, one for each day in a month. Whenever you have an assignment or other matter that requires attention at a later date, write a note to yourself on a small card, and place it in the proper folder. Every morning, check the folder for the day to ensure that an important duty is not forgotten. However, you must guard against continually refiling jobs for later attention. Make performance of jobs in the tickler file a *must.* For longer range planning, prepare a second file of 12 monthly folders, which can be utilized in similar fashion. For those who prefer a simpler system, the desk calendar memo is suggested.

Whatever system you use, be sure you follow up on assignments, promises made, appointments, etc. Ask yourself these questions:

Am I behind schedule on any old assignment? (If so, uncover the reason, and take steps to get on schedule.)

Have I made any promises that haven't been kept? (Fulfill them now. Remember that if you fail to perform a job for someone else you may hold up dozens of other people.)

What new jobs require attention? (Have a plan for getting them done on time.)

Before starting the day's work, review what you should accomplish before quitting time. You may want to make a list and cross off the items as they are completed. Do the most urgent assignment first. If two jobs are of equal importance,

TACKLE THE TOUGHEST ONE FIRST

tackle the tougher one first. That is the antidote for the natural human tendency to stall.

Assignments

As a supervisor, you are responsible not only for your own 2,880 minutes per week, more or less, but for 2,880 minutes multiplied by the number of people in your group. To save their time, as well as your own, give clear-cut instructions. Be sure employees understand what to do, how to do it, and where to obtain needed information. Before one job is completed, have another ready. Activity breeds ambition and progress; hesitation fosters idleness and laziness.

Some supervisors complain that they are overburdened with detail. Keep in mind the fact that a supervisor cannot afford to become entangled in too much routine work. The way to keep jobs from piling up on your desk is to assign them to someone who can handle them promptly. Unload simple jobs on your men so that you can spend adequate time on real problems that require more training and experience.

Production or Creative Work

Almost every supervisor personally does a certain amount of work of a creative nature. He needs time to develop efficient working methods and solve the tougher problems that arise.

In most industrial organizations, supervisors have the required ingenuity, experience, and technical knowledge. Their problem in doing creative work is either in finding time for it or in concentrating on the task at hand.

Interruptions due to your own work habits are the worst enemies of creative work. There is always a great deal of inertia in returning to a job you have left for a few minutes. Plan your

HELP THE OTHER FELLOW-HE'LL HELP YOU

own jobs as intelligently as you expect your men to plan theirs. Obtain all necessary information before you begin. Also, be certain that your men have been given such clear-cut assignments and definite responsibilities that they won't continually interrupt you on minor matters that they should handle themselves.

Correspondence

In writing letters, be brief; know the facts before starting. If a secretary handles your letters, allow her to take care of routine letters herself. An effective method of speeding letter writing, used by some men, is to blue-pencil the letter to be answered, noting significant points to be covered. A specific time of day should be allotted to correspondence.

Conferences with Superiors

Your supervisor's time is more valuable than your own. He will appreciate having you follow these rules:

1. Refer problems to him only when you can't handle them yourself.
2. Keep him informed on progress by *brief* oral reports or *brief* written reports. Have the entire story lined up before you go in to see him.

3. When assigned a job, get it straight the first time. Don't make it necessary for him to repeat it later.

Conferences with Other Groups

Cooperation with other groups is essential in all supervisory positions. When your job and that of another group *overlap*, keep in close contact so each one knows what the other is doing. You can save time for yourself and other groups by working together on mutual problems. True cooperation is a 50–50 deal. Help the other fellow, and he'll help you.

Too often, narrow-minded men are close-mouthed for fear someone else will get the credit. Remember that, if you have good ideas and perform excellent work, the boss will know it.

Contacts Outside Company

A certain amount of outside contact is desirable, especially in some types of jobs. However, the time should be spent profitably. The test is: Will such contacts save money or increase production?

Outside of working hours, it will profit a supervisor to join his technical or professional society and seek to learn from others doing similar work.

OUTSIDE CONTACT IS DESIRABLE

HOW TO PLAN A JOB

An efficient plan is always necessary, whether for a small job requiring a couple of hours or for one requiring months. In the first case, the plan may be in your mind; in the second, it should be on paper.

In scheduling any but the smallest jobs, the following plan for planning may be helpful:

1. Know what you want to accomplish.
2. Break a job into simple steps or parts.
3. Set a time schedule.
4. Assign parts of the job to those best suited.
5. Follow through, assembling the job and reviewing it to be sure the stated objectives are achieved.

State Your Objectives

A great railroad promoter once said of an unsuccessful road that it ran from "nowhere to nowhere." How often we tend to

DON'T WORK IN THE DARK

start a job without being exactly sure of its objective and the purpose for doing it. If you want results, don't work in the dark. Be certain of what you want to accomplish—in quality, in quantity, in what amount of time. If objectives and purposes are clear in your mind, you will find it easy to write them down in one or two sentences. The act of actually putting them in black and white often helps to crystallize your thinking.

Sometimes a supervisor says, "I've got a plan, but I can't put it down on paper. Too many details." But if you can't write it down, the chances are it isn't really a plan. Better review the situation and define your objectives more clearly.

Before starting the job, you will want to establish certain standards of quality, some of which may already have been set for you by company policy. A worker, for instance, knows that his work is expected to conform to standard company procedures. In some cases certain standards are set to suit a particular job, "trimmings" being eliminated in the interest of speed.

Break It Up

A long, complicated job often looks forbidding. You may feel like shoving it to one side because it looks hopeless. Thorough analysis, however, may show you that it can be broken up into simpler jobs.

Some jobs are most easily broken up into steps, which follow each other in order. A drafting supervisor, for instance, may sketch a drawing in rough form; a draftsman do the detail

OBTAIN NECESSARY INFORMATION

drawing; another man complete the lettering; a fourth man check it for accuracy. Through years of experience, many types of work have been broken down into routine steps and follow a definite procedure.

Many large jobs may be broken into parts that are done simultaneously. Obviously, if several people are working on a job, it can be done much more quickly than by the efforts of one person. Especially is this true if the different parts require varying types of experience and training.

With a definite course of action outlined, determine what additional information is needed to complete each portion of the job. Decide where the information is to be obtained—

TITLE	DRAFTSMAN	DAYS REQ'D.	EST. DRAFT. DATE	EST. CHECK. DATE	TO STRESS	FROM STRESS	FINISHED	COMMENTS
(1) LEADING EDGE SPAR ASSY.	MITCHEL WILKINS	13	10-18	10-18	10-19	10-20	10-17	3 SHEETS 1 SHEET TO BE REDRAWN
(2) FRONT SPAR ASS'Y.	COHEN KEUFFEL EDEN SHANON	15	10-19					
(3) END PLATE @ 44	RAMSBERG	2	10-19					
(4) END PLATE @ 479	HAVELIN VLODSKI	4	10-23					

PLANNING CHART used in scheduling and checking progress for layout and drawing work on a "rush" project. All drawings were listed on this chart, together with the 75 draftsmen and layout men working on the job, scheduled completion dates, and the actual dates that various stages of each drawing were finished. Comments on progress were listed in the right-hand column.

whether staff experts or your superior should be consulted; whether laboratory tests are required; whether literature should be consulted.

The time element is important throughout all stages of planning. At some point you must establish a definite time schedule.

Set a Schedule

In making up a schedule, two dates are most important: (1) starting time and (2) date required. The time at which each

step or part must be finished can be filled in to suit the nature of the work and the speed of each individual.

Determine definitely how much time each portion of the job requires, how much time it is worth while spending on each.

On some jobs there is no definite completion date that must be met. However, for your own good and that of your men, establish a goal, based on past experience on similar work. Don't hesitate to tell a man when a job is wanted. There is as much complaining about not enough work as about too much work.

While work is in process, check the schedule regularly to be certain that progress is being made and that the completion date will be met.

Make Assignments

It's a basic supervision principle that individuals be used to the best of their ability. In making assignments, you are faced with two alternatives:

1. Suit the job to the worker.
2. Suit the worker to the job.

The first procedure is always preferable. If you have a man fitted for a certain type of work, he should be assigned this

FIT THE JOB TO THE WORKER

work whenever possible. If you must fall back on the alternative, give special attention to training requirements during the planning stage, rather than wait until an untrained man has undertaken the job.

Follow Through

As each step or part of an assignment is finished, it requires thorough checking to ensure that it is "on the beam" and that it won't hold up future work. When all parts are complete, assemble them and review the entire job. Ask yourself these questions:

Are all details complete?

Are the stated objectives accomplished?

Have I conformed to company policies?

Have I conformed to standards established for this particular job?

Nothing is so embarrassing as turning in a completed job to your own boss, only to find that you have omitted an important item. By following through on a job, you can avoid such embarrassment and save your own time and that of your superior.

For best results, plan your work and work your plan.

14

Keeping Others Posted

"GET 'EM young, treat 'em rough, and don't tell 'em anything."

The boys down at the pool hall used to hand out this advice on women, and many an old-time boss used the same philosophy in handling his employees, as well.

There are still supervisors who don't tell their employees enough to enable them to do their jobs efficiently. Maybe such supervisors don't know any better. Perhaps they are afraid of losing their own jobs and seek security in a smoke screen of secrecy.

Most likely, though, they forget that *information is the life blood of industry.*

When free circulation of information throughout the business is obstructed, the entire organization suffers. Effectively circulated, whether by drawings, reports, discussions, or memoranda, adequate information results in proper functioning of all members of the organization, better understanding, more enthusiastic cooperation, and increased production.

In a small business, management and workers may have daily associations, and each finds it easy to understand the aims and problems of the other. In a large enterprise with highly specialized departments and groups, however, management and workers tend to be forced apart, despite the efforts of personnel experts and others to bring them closer together.

Many personnel problems resulting from bigness could probably be avoided if all concerned had the mutual understanding that comes with effective communication of ideas. It has been quite a while since the typical company executive was a worker himself. Concerned as he is with weighty problems, it is not surprising that he may have forgotten how the average worker thinks and feels. Likewise, the average worker is inclined to see every problem from his own viewpoint. Often, he finds it difficult to see a problem as it affects other groups in a company or the organization as a whole.

BRING MEN AND MANAGEMENT TOGETHER

It is the job of the supervisor—the man in the middle—to bring men and management together by keeping information circulating in three directions. He must

Keep employees posted.

Keep management posted.

Keep fellow supervisors posted.

That's quite a responsibility for a supervisor, but keeping others posted is an important part of every one of his activities.

Keeping Employees Posted

What do employees want to know? Well, they probably have an idle curiosity about many things that are none of their business, but they also have a laudable desire for a more than superficial knowledge of how a company operates, something of its future plans, the reasons behind major decisions, and the purpose of the projects on which they or their friends are working. They want to know how management feels about the problems facing the company. Such information may appear on the surface to be of no value to the average employee; yet, when he doesn't get it, he feels like an outsider. It cannot be expected that outsiders will contribute the loyalty, interest, and effort a supervisor needs in his team. It's to the supervisor that the employee looks for inside information and, if the supervisor himself doesn't have it, a little time spent in finding out would be justified.

IT MAY BE GREEK TO HIM

It is easy to subscribe to the smug theory that employees are happier if they are kept blissfully unaware of the reasons behind certain company rules and regulations which we regard as necessary evils. If the employee knows why the rule is necessary, however, chances are he is big enough and sufficiently tolerant to abide by it more cheerfully than we would suspect. Certainly, he should abide by rules without kicking, even if he doesn't know their purpose, but it's not human nature to do so. A person's natural inclination to tolerance cannot be enlisted without "reason why" enlightenment.

Certain information is needed by employees in performing their daily jobs. Experienced employees may need only a small amount of instruction and may be able to fill in gaps in information, but newer, less experienced persons need to be told a great many things.

To keep the new man from being in the dark, be sure you tell him everything he needs to know in order to complete his assignments quickly. Certain routine procedures and standard practices which are old stuff to you may be Greek to him. You don't have to furnish all the information yourself, but refrain from hoarding valuable data that will expedite the job. Be sure the employee knows where to go for the facts he needs. It is well to designate some older man in the group to whom he can go for help when you aren't available.

Keeping Management Posted

There's hardly a management decision that does not affect a number of employees in one way or another. If these decisions

A STONE WALL IS BUILT UP

do not take into account the sentiments of the workers, a stone wall is gradually built up between them and management. Management requires an intimate knowledge of employee attitudes, and it's up to the supervisor to see that this information is passed upward. Such information should be accurate and thorough, not distorted by the supervisor to serve his own interests. It's especially important that a supervisor inform his own boss about employee grievances when something can be done to correct them, before they build up into major problems.

Of as vital interest to your superiors as to your employees is the progress of each individual in your group. Promotions are being made nearly every day, and management wants them to go to people best suited to the jobs.

Some companies require that supervisors evaluate their employees periodically on merit-rating forms. If properly used, merit ratings are reasonably accurate in giving a continuous record of how an employee is getting along. Too often, however, a supervisor will manipulate his merit ratings to achieve certain things; for example, a raise in pay that he cannot justify unless he gives a rating that is puffed up. As a result, management is kept posted—but falsely. It is just as undesirable to rate a mediocre man too high as to rate an excellent man too low. Any deliberate attempt to beat the system is unfair to all others in the group.

Just as you need to know how jobs in your group are progressing, so does management, though in more general terms. Although your superior doesn't want to be bothered with petty details (or, at least, shouldn't be). he does want to know the

KEEP OTHERS POSTED

progress of each job, the expected completion dates, and accounts of unusual or difficult problems. Such reports require discrimination by the supervisor in picking out significant facts and disregarding those that are irrelevant.

Keeping Other Supervisors Posted

As part of your duty to keep others informed, "deal in" your fellow supervisors on any matter that affects them and their work. It's well to keep them posted by (1) forwarding copies of important memoranda and reports; (2) discussing mutual problems as soon as they arise; (3) informing them of progress on jobs on which they will do or are doing some work; (4) exchanging friendly information whenever desirable.

Two Rules

Boiled down, the duty of *keeping others posted* can be expressed as two rules:

> Keep men and management informed on each other's progress, plans, thoughts, problems, and feelings.
>
> Keep all interested people adequately informed on the progress of your group's work, including special problems and new developments.

WRITING IT RIGHT

File it in the wastebasket if it doesn't have guts!

The purpose of a memorandum to your boss or other associates is to transmit information. If it doesn't do this completely, accurately, and briefly, you might as well throw it away. Reports and instructions that raise more questions than they answer aren't worth the paper they're printed on. Common gripes against instructions and reports are the following:

- Too long
- Incomplete
- Arranged in disorderly fashion
- Unconvincing
- Too many side issues
- Pass the buck
- Vague and confusing
- Contradictory

Poor grammar

Misplaced statistics and charts

Writers of memoranda might well take a lesson from a Negro preacher who explains his success as an orator as follows:

"Fust, Ah tells 'em what Ah's gonna' tell 'em.
"Then, Ah tells 'em.
"Finally, Ah tells 'em what Ah told 'em."

Put in more academic style, this adds up to (1) introduction, (2) body, (3) conclusion; or the *why*, the *what*, and the *wherefore* of your communication.

Quick Getaway

Why write half a page before you say anything? Tell your reader something vital *right at the start*. Your very first sentence

SELL YOUR IDEA AT THE BEGINNING

or paragraph should specifically define the problem and tell why your memo was written. The reader then knows right away whether or not he should be interested in reading further. Sell your idea at the beginning before the reader goes to sleep.

Include a *brief* digest of your conclusions or recommendations in the introduction. If you're not ashamed of your conclusions, why bury them in a maze of words and phrases in the middle of the report? Let your reader in on the secret right off the bat. He will then look at the problem from your viewpoint as he reads the rest of your memorandum. He will analyze your statements to see whether or not they back up the solution which you offer.

Be brief, however, or your reader will set your communication aside to read at some convenient time. (And it's never convenient to read a long, rambling letter.)

Go Heavy on Facts

A memorandum must have plenty of guts; that is, pertinent facts that support your conclusions and recommendations.

MANY PEOPLE WILL HOLD YOUR OPINIONS WORTHLESS

Many people will hold your opinions worthless unless you can substantiate them with authentic data. Arrange these data in a clear-cut, logical manner. Put first things first, keeping in mind the reader's needs and questions. You will be more apt to do this if you follow a prearranged outline, no matter whether the outline is in your head, neatly typed on bond paper, or scribbled on the back of an envelope.

If you're wise, you won't clutter up your memos with rambling discussions of side issues, defenses of past actions, and supplementary material that has no bearing on the problem.

Supporting charts, tables, or other exhibits have no place in the middle of a memo. Place them in an appendix at the end of your communication where they can be readily referred to by those readers who demand full proof.

Have a Conclusion

A memo should lead to some sort of a conclusion, suggestion, request, opinion, or summary of information. Don't let your thoughts dangle in mid-air. Use the final paragraph to bring them down to earth. It's your last chance to reach the reader and, as such, should leave him with a clear-cut idea of what he has read.

Furnish the Proof

If you have test data, drawings, or other documents that back up your conclusions, include them as attachments or appendices.

The casual reader may simply glance over your report and pay special attention to your first and last paragraphs. But the man who is deeply interested will not be so easily satisfied. He will want to assure himself beyond the shadow of a doubt that your statements are correct. Don't let this important reader down. Give him the facts. If he doesn't get them in your communication, he'll either turn you down or waste time in getting the essential data by other methods.

Check for Contents

It will be worth your time to review your first draft carefully and make certain the requirements are fulfilled.

Does the memorandum answer fully and accurately the questions that led to writing it? Will it lead to the desired action on the part of the reader? If not, review your statements and edit or rewrite as required.

Does it contain enough facts and supporting data to be accurate and convincing? Your superior and employees may trust your opinions, but how about the other people who don't know your ability but who read your report? Adequate supporting data are necessary so that the reader can evaluate your conclusions and check them with his own.

Double-check for Readership

Though your memo may contain valuable information, if no one reads it you have wasted your time. And if it's poorly written but nevertheless read by someone, you have wasted the reader's time. Be sure you interest your readers by following these four rules:

1. Make it significant.
2. Be brief.
3. Emphasize the new.
4. Be logical and convincing.

Make your memo mean something to the reader. If it will save him time and money, say so, not in general terms, but specifically. The more significant or meaningful a memo is to a reader, the better chance you have to get the results you want.

Abraham Lincoln said a man's legs need be only long enough to reach the ground. Likewise, memos and reports need be only

BE LOGICAL AND CONVINCING

long enough to reach a satisfactory solution. Anything beyond this is superfluous.

Remember that nothing is as old as yesterday's newspaper or last year's ideas. There's no need to spend a great deal of time on the obvious. Stress the new methods and ideas which you propose as a solution to the problem under consideration.

Above all, be logical and convincing. Include sufficient proof for your statements. Give facts, figures, specific instances, reasons why—all of which ensure readership.

If your memo has been written, not from your own standpoint, but that of *the reader*, don't worry. You will have aroused his interest in the very beginning; you will have included all the facts he needs; and finally, you will have wrapped up the entire memo in a concluding paragraph for his convenience. The reader will be better off after reading a well-written memo, and so will you.

15

Selling Ideas

As a supervisor, there is no reason why you cannot be a good seller of ideas, and there is every reason why you must be a good salesman.

No matter how well a new design, method, or idea has been worked out, it will require all your ingenuity as a salesman to present it effectively.

Too often, the man with a half-baked idea is able to put it across because he is well versed in salesmanship. Such a person is like the high-pressure door-to-door peddler who sells housewives some tricky gadget that looks good but doesn't last very long. Naturally, he doesn't try coming back to the same place for a repeat sale.

On the other hand, the man with a good idea is often unable to convince his boss or associates of its worth. When others less familiar with the subject cannot immediately see the advantage of his plan, he tends to become annoyed and discouraged.

It is not enough merely to have a good "product"—in your case a time- or money-saving idea. You must be able to convince your boss and the management of the value of your plan so that you can secure their wholehearted approval. You also need to sell your fellow supervisors so that they will cooperate with you to the utmost advantage for the company. What's more, in order to build enthusiasm in your group, you will have to sell each individual member on the importance of his role in carrying out the idea.

Since your work is based on facts, figures, tests, and analysis, it is obvious that you will want to employ the "reasoning" sales technique. That is, you should present your idea clearly; then back it up with facts that answer definitely and authoritatively any objections that may be offered.

Although logical reasoning is often your best method of attack, you should not ignore other sales appeals such as job pride, ambition, desire for praise, loyalty, competitive spirit, love of publicity. Sometimes, these are the straws that break the

camel's back—the appeals that cause one idea to be accepted and another one to be rejected.

In putting over an idea, there are four brief rules:

1. Gain attention.
2. Arouse interest.
3. Create conviction and desire.
4. Secure action.

The entire art of selling ideas is wrapped up in attention, interest, conviction, desire, and action.

Gain Attention by Showing a Need

In order to attract attention for a good idea, you must be certain of two things: (1) that there is a definite need for the idea and (2) that this need is made clear to the prospect.

If your idea is of benefit to yourself alone, you will probably have a difficult time selling it. On the other hand, the more it is needed by the other fellow—and the organization to which he belongs—the better are your chances of making a sale. It is, therefore, well to forget yourself and concentrate on the other fellow's requirements. Make a careful analysis of the present situation and know the problem so thoroughly that you will have no trouble in explaining why your plan is desirable.

GAIN ATTENTION

At this point, provoke curiosity by mentioning that you have an idea with certain advantages. But avoid overselling at the beginning, lest you kill your "follow-through." Resist the temptation to tell all the details hurriedly a few minutes before your customer is due to leave for lunch or another appointment. Instead, be sure you have the prospect's undivided attention at a time when he is not up to his neck in work that will keep your idea from getting careful consideration.

There are some days and times when he will not be in a favorable mood to listen to your story. On a Monday, for example, most people are either getting readjusted to work after a week end of relaxation or are so preoccupied with their own problems that they are not receptive to new ideas. Likewise, there are certain periods during a day when the men to whom you must sell your ideas will be busily engaged in such work as planning or dictation. Avoid trying to sell your ideas at such times, since you will not attract enough attention to proceed to the next step of arousing interest.

Make Your Story Arouse Interest

Once you have shown the need for your idea and have the prospect's undivided attention, present your case briefly, but completely. It is important that you demonstrate just how the problem is solved by your plan. Be sure the prospect has sufficient background material to understand thoroughly both the problem and the solution.

In order to get the prospect in a favorable mood, open your sales talk with the most obvious advantage of your plan—the one with which he is apt to agree without much discussion.

Next, present the major advantage—the basic selling point that should create acceptance for your idea. This outstanding benefit will probably be the one to solve the main problem that led to the presentation of your idea. In the case of a new product design, it may be one of the following:

- Improved operation
- Easier maintenance
- Better weight
- Sturdier construction
- Easier manufacture
- Time saving
- Money saving
- Safety
- Eye appeal
- Comfort
- Marketability
- Competitive advantage

Compare your plan with others and show points of superiority. Demonstrate how it averts trouble and does away with disadvantages of older methods.

It is also well to encourage the "prospect" to contribute

modifications of your idea, particularly if he is the type that likes to originate everything himself. If he feels that it is also his idea, or partly so, he will be more apt to approve it. Be sure he keeps agreeing with you, point by point, and gets in the habit of saying "yes."

KEEP HIM AGREEING WITH YOU

Telling your story and stressing the advantages should have aroused plenty of interest in your idea. However, you must also convince him that the idea is sound and free from "bugs."

Present Proof

Clear-cut exposition of your plan will not always be enough to prove your point. Frequently, the prospect will tend to be conservative because of a fear of the unknown and untried. To build confidence in your plan you may therefore have to use every sales argument at your command.

If a similar idea has been used successfully, tell when and where. If you are backed up by the opinions of others, say so. If published articles substantiate your case, present them as part of your argument.

Avoid generalities. Give specific facts, figures, and examples. Use photographs, charts, and tables that prove your points.

Don't be afraid to mention possible objections to your plan—but have reasonable solutions prepared.

By all means, emphasize your main idea, stating it at least three times in positive, definite terms.

GIVE SPECIFIC FACTS, FIGURES, ETC.

Secure Action

As part of your plan, include the specific suggested action which you desire. Sometimes, especially if you have presented a clear-cut case, you can secure immediate results. Often, however, you will want to give the prospect plenty of time to think it over. Even in such an instance, it is well to secure some preliminary action that will bring you nearer the final goal.

Perhaps the preliminary action will be one of the following:

A statement that the matter will be reviewed and a decision reached at some specific time.

Approval for a test or trial or development work.

A statement that the matter will be discussed with others who are affected by the plan.

If you are really sold on your idea, you will not allow it to die. Follow up at an appointed time to get definite results. Only when you have secured the desired action has your salesmanship been effective.

16

Cooperator and Cooperatee

COOPERATION, like children, should be seen rather than heard; like charity, it should begin at home; like the quality of mercy, it blesses him that gives and him that receives.

Defined[1] as "working together willingly and intelligently to achieve a common purpose," cooperation calls for *action*, not talk. In fact, much talk about cooperation often indicates a lack of it. When it permeates an organization, however, the cooperative attitude becomes a part of the operation, and the chances are it gets less than its due share of credit for smooth, efficient production.

Cooperation should not be looked upon as a favor to be bestowed upon friends or traded for favors received. Neither is it a service to be performed grudgingly under compulsion. Rather, cooperation is an essential part of the job an individual is paid for doing. The cooperative effort expected from an individual is generally described by the duties and responsibilities of his job; but the degree of his cooperation—the willingness and sincerity with which he participates—has no more of a defined ceiling than honesty or loyalty. The man who cooperates is giving no more than can be reasonably expected. The man who refuses to cooperate is giving less than is due.

So natural is the spirit of teamwork that much of our business is transacted in a friendly, cooperative manner, with little thought as to who is giving and who is getting. But while people are naturally cooperative, they also are naturally competitive. This latter trait sometimes crops up in misdirected aggressive-

[1] Spriegel, William R., and Edward Schulz, *Elements of Supervision*, John Wiley & Sons, Inc., New York, 1942.

ness and narrowness of purpose, which are downright uncooperative. Other factors contributing to noncooperation are fear, incompetence, personal animosity, feelings of inferiority, or failure to understand the objectives of a group.

Often, uncooperativeness is a rebuff to unwarranted, illogical, or indefinite demands. In this class fall repeated requests for special consideration needed to cover up a bad job or a needlessly

PEOPLE ARE NATURALLY COOPERATIVE

delayed production schedule; unreasonable demands for rush jobs that ignore more important work; vague or incomplete information that places an unnecessary burden on the cooperator; and the seemingly innocent little items that overnight mushroom into jobs of unforeseen size.

The responsibility for promoting cooperation falls equally upon the party who asks and the party who gives, hereinafter known as the *cooperatee* and the *cooperator*, respectively. And it begins with the cooperatee.

Getting Cooperation

When you have a problem that seems to require outside aid and cooperation, break it down to determine just what part of the work you can do and what, specifically, is required outside.

Select carefully the prospective cooperator or cooperators.

In making a selection, look at the problem from the other fellow's viewpoint. Is the job within his field of activity or responsibility? If not, it is possible that you should ask someone else for help, or do it yourself. Once in a while you may discover that the job has no place in the program at all.

When you have selected the proper cooperator, you undertake certain responsibilities as cooperatee.

Plan the job as a complete unit so that it will not be necessary to run back with some "extras" after the cooperator thinks his part is finished.

THE "NONCOOPERATOR"

As far as possible, without trying to "run his business," determine how your job can be adapted to the cooperator's personnel, equipment, and program.

Present the request in a straightforward, complete manner, giving sufficient background for proper comprehension and enough "reason why" to establish the need. Remember, this is business. So unless your request is unwarranted, unreasonable, vague, or incomplete, no apology is required of the cooperatee.

But don't just dump the job in his lap and run. Provide any additional information, advice, or help requested by the cooperator.

When arrangements have been mutually agreed upon and it is thoroughly understood *who is to do what when*, it is almost mandatory that the cooperatee get out of the cooperator's hair and stay out until the job is delivered or the completion date arrives. Unnecessary meddling is likely to turn an otherwise agreeable cooperator into a mulish noncooperator.

After the cooperator has turned in his work, the cooperatee still has an important obligation to fulfill in the matter of credit. Give full recognition for assistance rendered by other persons or groups. Remember, management is on the lookout for executives who are good cooperatees.

Giving Cooperation

Unless your knowledge, ability, or organization is pitifully meager, you are probably called upon, from time to time, to act as cooperator. When you are thus honored, you incur certain obligations. First, as in the case of the cooperatee, scrutinize the job carefully to determine if you are best fitted to take it on. If it is necessary and can be fitted legitimately into your program, it's your job. However, do not be so eager to get your fingers into a bigger pie that you undertake jobs for which other persons or groups would be much better suited.

After you have agreed to do the job, treat it as you would your own. Be sure you obtain all necessary information. Usually it's well to get a specific dead line to forestall last-minute rushes and misunderstandings.

Complete all the work you have agreed to do. It's not wise to dump part of it back to the cooperatee when he least expects it. As cooperator, you're not ultimately responsible for the job, so turn it out as the cooperatee wants it. Remember, you're simply doing your duty, not a great personal favor.

After the job is completed, accept gracefully what credit is due, but don't bother to sprinkle a few hints as to how you helped the guy out of a hole. People would rather give recognition freely than under duress.

Joint Efforts

Some projects are of such scope that many persons or groups are assigned to the job. In such cases, several persons or groups may be equally responsible individually, and also collectively, for the successful completion of the job. Each is at once a cooperatee and a cooperator, since the work must be highly integrated.

Joint efforts of this nature require teamwork to the *n*th

degree, both within and among groups. Effectiveness of the combined operation depends upon appreciation and execution of obligations by both cooperatee and cooperator.

Usually there is a competitive feeling in such cases, which is not necessarily unhealthy. Paradoxical as it may seem, friendly

competition, if it is confident and competent, may thrive side by side with cooperation.

The Diplomacy of Cooperation

As practiced by a supervisor, cooperation must be up, down, and sideways. It's fairly easy to work in harmony with your subordinates and your boss since your mutual interests are quite apparent, and there are many opportunities for friendly contacts. "Sideways" cooperation—with fellow supervisors—is somewhat harder to secure. Jealousies, fears of being overshadowed, and unfriendly attitudes destroy a man's ability to be either a cooperatee or a cooperator. Good, sincere diplomacy—not to be confused with skulduggery—can be used to great advantage.

There's no need to wait for the other person to indicate a desire to cooperate. Get to know and understand him by being friendly and taking an interest in his problems, especially those that overlap your own.

When supervisors run into antagonism, jealously, and coolness, they often do the very things that decrease cooperation. They shun contacts with the "opposition," write unfriendly memoranda, do a lot of idle talking, but take no action. Best practice in building teamwork is to multiply your contacts with the unfriendly person. Go out of your way to call him or see him whenever there is something to be ironed out. You won't agree on many things, and there may be spirited discussions. But if you are fair and open-minded, the other fellow will recognize the fact and the chance for compromise is increased.

MENTALLY SEAT YOURSELF AT HIS DESK

Since everyone is inclined to be in love with his own ideas and methods, if you want to secure cooperation, don't be always right. It isn't humanly possible. Do a job the other fellow's way if it's the better way or if it makes no real difference in the end. Most persons like to be asked for suggestions, especially if you are sincere and unprejudiced.

Don't blame others for not getting on your band wagon with the same enthusiasm you have. But you can generate some enthusiasm if you develop the "you" attitude. Think in terms of the other fellow's department as well as your own. Mentally seat yourself at his desk, and you'll probably discover that you have a common goal, though approached from different viewpoints.

Many of your associates would be glad to cooperate with you on a problem if it were not for one thing: The extra effort may interfere with their own work. This calls for good timing on your part. In initiating any cooperative venture, choose a time when the other group is not up to its neck in work. And show how it is to their benefit to allot time to the venture.

Certain actions and personality traits tend to hinder co-operation. While ridding yourself of such traits, it is well to be tolerant of them in others. Typical of the things that lead to

AVOID DOMINEERING ATTITUDE

antagonism are always having an alibi; failure to keep promises; jealousy; domineering attitude; buck passing; "political" maneuvering. Most of these can be traced back to a habit of thinking too much about our own selfish interests and not enough about those of other people and the common purpose of a group. If the time some people spent as politicians, trying to build up their personal influence, were devoted to extra work, the resulting recognition received would be greater, more lasting, more satisfying.

Show Appreciation

When your associates go out of their way to cooperate, they will appreciate a word of thanks. But, more than that, they will be proud of a job well done and will welcome any credit you give them in talks with their associates and superiors.

17

Get the Boys Together

A CONFERENCE can often get nowhere faster than any other form of human cooperative effort."

So says Cartoonist Don Herold, author of *How to Harness a Conference*, who believes that conferences shouldn't be monkey business since they are expensive when you add up the salaries involved.

"There is no reason why 12 men in a room should add up dumber than any one of the 12," he says. "Twelve men in a room ought to be at least 12 times as smart as any one of them.

If managed the right way, 12 men in a room should stimulate, rather than nullify, each other. *That* is the *ideal* for a conference."

Some conferences, however, are no more productive than the good old-fashioned bull session where men gather to discuss golf or politics or religion. In fact, many a conference degenerates into a bull session when not kept in hand.

If they are so easily sidetracked, you may ask, are such meetings or conferences desirable? People evidently think so, or they wouldn't be calling so many of them.

"Let's get together and settle this thing," is something we've heard many a time. It happens when a new method is recommended; or a man is recommended for promotion to a vacancy; or a contract is awarded for purchase of equipment.

The idea is good. Modern industry is so complex its problems cannot be handled by a single man. It requires the combined experience and judgment of hundreds of specialists. The common meeting ground for their ideas is the conference, whether held in an oak-paneled director's room, in the corner of a machine shop, or in a busy office.

A lot of people have talked and written a lot about the kind of conference that is held in a conference room, complete with spittoons and ash trays.

However, the most common type of conference has been ignored.

That is the kind which occurs when two or three men are huddled over a table or seated around a desk with the idea of settling a problem.

Such a meeting has the same purpose as a more formal conference. Since it has no designated leader, however, it is just as easily turned into a nonproductive, bickering gripe fest or bull session as the other type. Which is saying a lot, when you consider how easy it is to get a formal confab sidetracked. Remember that the rules which will be given for a formal conference also apply to an informal get-together, with certain details omitted.

Regardless of time, place, or size, a successful conference is usually a well-planned conference.

How to Plan a Conference

The first step in planning a conference is to be certain you have a justified purpose in arranging it. Is there a definite problem? Will the conferees be able to contribute to its solution? Is the solution worth the time of those who will attend?

It's important to have a conference plan, even if the plan consists of a few notes scribbled on the back of an envelope. Determine beforehand how you will introduce the problem (briefly, of course). List the points to be covered in the discussion, the questions to be brought up, the possible conclusions that may be reached.

GET THE RIGHT PEOPLE TOGETHER

A clear picture of questions to be answered will help you select the right people to get together. However, that doesn't mean keeping opposing factions from meeting. You can't act like a dinner hostess who never invites Mrs. Uppington and Mrs. Van Astorbilt to the same affair because they don't agree. Conferences are called to iron out differences, to compromise varying viewpoints in order to arrive at a mutually satisfying conclusion. If you want really to solve your problem, include representatives of every different viewpoint that is concerned with it. Above all, be sure that you and the conference members bring to the meeting the information needed in solving the problem.

Physical arrangements are important. Reserve a conference room well ahead of time. Be sure there are enough chairs. A blackboard often helps line up ideas and is invaluable in keeping on the beam. Notify the conferees well in advance in writing, and insist that the conference begin on time.

The Open-minded Attitude

You can't get results in a conference, large or small, when some people come to it with stubborn, closed minds. It's essential, too, that the leader conduct the discussion in a fair, impartial, open-minded manner.

There are certain attitudes that you should leave at home when joining a conference:

The attitude that you won't learn anything from others.

The attitude that you are right, and no one can convince you otherwise.

The attitude that you are expecting to be done an injustice by others in the conference.

The attitude that the blame for an action should be focused on a victim.

Come to a conference with an open mind—with a determination to give and take, to examine a problem from all sides, to unearth every pertinent fact, to arrive at a conclusion that will satisfy the objective of the meeting.

Have an Objective

It sounds elementary to say "Have an objective." If there weren't an objective, why was the conference called?

WHY WAS A CONFERENCE CALLED

We often wonder why some conferences are called. The trouble with some of them is that they have too many objectives—as many as there are people getting together.

Someone has got to have the conferees decide on a goal at the very start. In a formal conference, this is the chairman's job. In an informal get-together, someone must take the initiative and get the others off to the right start with a brief clearly stated objective. With this done, you can get down to business.

Keep on the Beam

Once a confab has begun, it's no easy job to keep it on the beam. There are too many byways of discussion that can be followed, and too many people who are willing to let things drift aimlessly.

Keep the main consideration foremost. Don't allow a maze of details to make a haze of an important problem.

Get all the facts that bear on your problem. Obtain expressions of opinion from all viewpoints, not just from one or two people who like to hear themselves talk. Repress talkative individuals, especially yourself. The conference leader's remarks should probably be no more than 15 to 20 per cent of the total. Gain the confidence of the group by being impartial, by suppressing your own opinions, and by directing the discussion at the main issues.

COME WITH COOPERATIVE ATTITUDES

If you're the leader, you shouldn't think for the members of the conference. Let them do their own thinking. Avoid acting like a professor. Your job is to stimulate and guide the conference, not to give a lecture.

Differences of opinion are bound to arise. When they do, they should be considered in an impersonal way. Perhaps the differences may be traced to the use of the same words with varying meanings, or to disagreement on minor rather than major items, or to personal suspicions and resentments.

It's not wise to bury controversial issues and get everyone to agree on some nicely phrased, innocuous generality. Drag the controversy into the open. Define the controversial factors. Obtain all necessary information for reaching an agreement. Weigh *all* the facts in the light of the stated objectives.

The leader can use well-timed questions in directing the discussion, stimulating thought, and encouraging shy people to participate. However, it's not good practice to put people on the spot by asking direct questions such as "Mr. X, what do you think?" Make the conference so interesting that everyone will be eager to participate.

- At intervals, sum up the discussion. Thus, you will dispose of matters already completed and steer the conference toward unsolved portions of the problem. Many conference leaders have found that use of a blackboard for noting principal points is helpful in guiding conference thought. If it's more convenient, just jot down notes on paper as the meeting progresses. The blackboard outline or penciled notes will come in handy in summarizing the results of the conference and moving toward a conclusion.

Arrive at a Conclusion

After the problem has been given due consideration, a slight (or heavy) fog may permeate the meeting. The next step is to clear the air by arriving at a conclusion that integrates the best ideas that have been brought to light, a solution which achieves the stated objectives but does not have the disadvantages of other solutions previously proposed but proved unsatisfactory.

Beware of agreements that are fundamentally disagreements when you get below the surface. Your conclusion must be a sound one that will stand the test of being put to use. After completion of the conference, boil down the essential findings and report them to the conferees for their records. Be sure you and each person attending the conference know exactly what has been accomplished, just what is to be done by each one in carrying out the solution of the problem.

18

The Man Above

Just as cooperation between you and your subordinates is necessary for efficient production in your team, the fullest possible cooperation between you and the man above—your own boss—is essential to smooth operation of the entire department.

You need the friendship, respect, and confidence of your superior, because he is one step above you on the management ladder and therefore more familiar with the directives and policies of management.

He needs your friendship, respect, and confidence because you are a step lower on the same ladder and therefore more intimately acquainted with the individual worker.

Mutual friendship, respect, and confidence are the keys to good relations between you and your boss and other representatives of management.

Be a Balance Wheel

As a supervisor, it is your obligation to be a balance wheel between the viewpoints of both men and management. If you happen to be a spineless "yes" man, the chances are you are leaning too much toward the management viewpoint. Such

BOSSES DO NOT LIKE "NO-MEN"

practice may flatter your boss's ego for a brief while, but in the long run you lose his respect. On the other hand, if you are a "no" man, always finding fault with the boss's policies and directives, you may eventually lose his confidence. "Yes" men and "no" men are equally disliked and mistrusted. We need front-line supervisors with open minds, men who are capable of sizing up a situation and providing a workable solution. Your "yes" and "no" should signify an honest opinion and be coupled with intelligent suggestions.

It is well to remember that your problems, however difficult, are simpler than those of your chief. Although you are responsible for the work of only one or a small number of groups, he is responsible for two or three or four times as many groups, perhaps more. Having climbed to a higher position, the boss is paid more for what he knows rather than for what he does. Some years ago, he was in your shoes, confronted with the same problems you now face. His decisions are therefore based on longer experience, more comprehensive knowledge, and a broader outlook than you have yet gained. Whether or not you agree with his decisions, the viewpoints of your superior merit respect.

Foremost in maintaining good relations between you and the boss is a sincere desire on your part to carry out his instructions.

Carry Out Orders

The boss happens to be boss because management has confidence in his ability to plan and issue instructions that can be carried out. It is your job to execute his orders accurately and in detail, or to present reasons why they should be modified for better results. Too often, the inexperienced supervisor spends a great deal of time trying to find out why a job can't be done the boss's way, rather than trying to uncover methods of making the boss's plans work.

When you receive orders, it is probable that they are more general than those you give your subordinates. It is assumed that you have an understanding and appreciation of the over-all objectives, policies, and trends of your program. The boss may not make his directives detailed because he feels the need for having the benefit of your thinking and experience. Occasionally, he may not even know what he wants, and hence finds it impossible to be specific.

In such a case, what can you do?

Perhaps the "playback" technique will provide an answer. When you make a recording of your voice, it is possible to play the record back and hear your own voice. You can act as a playback for your chief. After he has given his instructions, repeat them in your own words.

"As I understand it," you may say, "what you want me to do is . . . ."

Not only does this enable you to restate the objectives and outline the procedure clearly, but it gives you an opportunity to inject some of your own ideas. If these ideas are good, the boss will no doubt agree with you and say "That is just what I want," even though it may not have occurred to him in the beginning. What's more, his opinion of your ability will probably be considerably enhanced.

Any differences in opinion should be ironed out at this time to keep you from going off on a tangent. Get a settlement on controversial matters before you waste man-hours. In such discussions, avoid arguments and display of temper that may lead

AVOID ARGUMENTS

to rash statements you can't back up. He who wins an argument loses it.

When a job has been assigned, it is of course your full responsibility. The extent to which you can handle it without intimate supervision determines your worth to the company. An executive was asked why two supervisors, seemingly at the same level, were paid widely different salaries. He explained, "They both receive the same amount of the company's money. One, however, takes such a great deal of my time, which is worth money, that I can't afford to make his salary check as large."

Although the boss does not want to be annoyed with trivialities, he does want to be kept fully informed about the progress you and your group are making.

Keep the Boss Informed

Just how much should the boss be kept informed about your work? A good rule to follow is the "exception" principle. When things are going well, your report to the boss might be something like this: "Everything's fine on the rush job. We're 50 per cent finished. Should have it done Thursday." Only if an *exceptional* problem arises will the boss be interested in a more detailed report. The boss should, however, have up-to-the-minute information on each job so that he can, in turn, make intelligent reports to his own superior.

Since the boss does not have so many contacts with the workers as you do, he will depend on you to keep him informed on the difficulties they face and how they feel about working conditions, policies, etc. If any of your subordinates are doing excellent work, it should be called to the chief's attention, preferably in the worker's presence.

From time to time, you'll probably make mistakes. If these are caught by someone else, you may be called on the carpet with more vengeance than if you frankly admit your errors to the boss. In the latter case, you have his sympathy and assistance in correcting the mistakes.

Lengthy defenses of your actions, however, are annoying to the boss, who is not interested in your efforts to "save face." Alibis are so distasteful that they should be avoided like poison. State the facts. Period!

Be Loyal

As long as you are working for a man he deserves your loyalty. If you find it impossible to give him this loyalty, it would be far better for you to sever connections (but not friendship).

Too often, we criticize our bosses, the management, and the company in order to make ourselves look good by comparison. Griping of this sort may mean we are not equal to our jobs. Psychologists say we tend to criticize people most severely when they demonstrate faults that are most glaring in our own personalities.

It is better to give the boss your support in recognition of his good qualities than to tear him down because of his weaknesses. However, you should not be blind to the chief's good and bad qualities. If you study him and really get to know him, you'll find he has some of each. You'll realize that he is very much a human being, with likes and dislikes, prejudices, and desires similar to those of anyone else.

By observing the boss's successful methods, you will be learning much that you can put to use yourself. By watching his weaknesses, you can compensate for them by relieving him of work for which you are better suited. A good subordinate will

DON'T WITHHOLD INFORMATION

supplement his boss to result in an effective combination of talents.

It is loyal, not disloyal, to study and train yourself to take the boss's job when he is ready for promotion. At the same time, you will want to train an understudy who can take your place. A big mistake made by some supervisors is to withhold information from their workers as if they were afraid of losing their jobs. Don't become too indispensable in your present job if you want to pave the way for promotion.

The supervisor with an apparently weak boss may be tempted to go over his head, thereby violating the straight-line principle of organization procedure. Remember that in going over the boss's head you show lack of confidence in him and indicate that you do not respect conventional procedure. Anything you may gain by going over his head is probably offset by the ill will you create.

If it is necessary to see the man above the man directly above you on a major problem, it is best to inform your boss what you are doing and secure his approval. Usually it is well to have a working understanding on this subject to cover "when" and "when not" under ordinary circumstances.

Make Suggestions

If you are a supervisor with initiative and imagination, you'll no doubt have a number of suggestions to make concerning new

IT'S WISE TO "SLEEP" ON NEW IDEAS

methods, new plans, or new ideas. That is a vital part of your job. Good suggestions are welcomed if they provide a sound method of solving a problem. Suggestions should not be mere "curbstone" opinions or hare-brained ideas, but based on accurate facts and mature consideration. It is wise to sleep on any new idea which you want to present, as a safeguard against jumping to conclusions.

Present your ideas at a time when the boss can give them his fullest consideration. Furnish him with sufficient background material so that he can understand the proposal offered and see that it meets a specific need. Give him plenty of time to think it over, and refrain from continually nagging him on the subject.

Since consideration of new ideas necessarily takes up a great deal of the boss's time, he will appreciate it if you refrain from suggesting any wild idea which you think will make an impression on him. Make your suggestions so good that whenever you have any to offer you are assured of an interested audience. A good test for a suggestion: Would *I* accept it if I were in his shoes?

Management's Obligations

In return for loyalty, respect, and confidence, there are certain things which the supervisor, in turn, can expect from management. The following are suggested by C. Donald Dallas,[1] president of the Revere Copper & Brass Company, Inc.:

"To be kept fully informed about what is going on.

"To be notified well in advance before a policy is put into effect.

"Support for his decisions.

"To be called in on departmental and interdepartmental conferences.

"Impartial praise and constructive criticism.

"To be made answerable to as few men with authority over him as possible.

"To expect fair pay—more remuneration than his subordinates receive—a chance for merited promotions; clear-cut instructions; and no buck-passing."

[1] From "The Foremen's Role in Management," *Supervision*, September, 1943.

19

Theory of Completed Staff Work

HALF-BAKED ideas, confusing reports, poorly checked work, hazy memoranda—all lead to inefficient production.

No job can be considered complete until it has been thoroughly investigated from every angle, prepared in workmanlike fashion, reviewed in the light of its objectives, checked and double-checked to eliminate errors.

The "theory of completed staff work" is given in an order issued by the U.S. Army's Provost Marshal General, dated January, 1942, published in the *Officer's Guide*. Though intended for staff officers, it expresses fundamental principles that can be applied in civilian industry and is of particular interest to supervisors and those in staff positions.

"*Complete staff work,*" says the Provost Marshal General, "is the study of a problem, and presentation of a solution, by a staff officer, in such form that all that remains to be done on the part of the head of the staff division, or the commander, is to indicate his approval or disapproval of the *completed action.* The words *completed action* are emphasized because the more difficult the problem is, the more the tendency is to present the problem to the chief in piece-meal fashion. It is your duty as a staff officer to work out the details. You should not consult your chief in the determination of those details, no matter how perplexing they may be. You may and should consult other staff officers. The product, whether it involves the pronouncement of a new policy or affects an established one, should when presented to the chief for approval or disapproval, be worked out in finished form.

"The impulse which often comes to the inexperienced staff officer to ask the chief what to do, recurs more often when the problem is difficult. It is accompanied by a feeling of mental frustration. It is so easy to ask the chief what to do, and it appears so easy for him to answer. Resist that impulse. You will succumb to it only if you do not know your job. It is your job to advise your chief what he ought to do, not to ask him what you ought to do. He needs answers, not questions. Your job is to study, write, restudy and rewrite until you have evolved a single proposed action—the best one of all you have considered. Your chief merely approves or disapproves.

"Do not worry your chief with long explanations and memoranda. Writing a memorandum to your chief does not constitute completed staff work, but writing a memorandum for your chief to send to someone else does. . . . The theory of completed staff work does not preclude a rough draft but the rough draft must not be a half-baked idea. . . .

"The *completed staff work* theory may result in more work for the staff officer, but it results in more freedom for the chief. This is as it should be. Further, it accomplishes two things:

a. **The chief is protected from half-baked ideas, voluminous memoranda, and immature oral presentments.**

b. **The staff officer who has a real idea to sell is enabled more readily to find a market.**

"When you have finished your *completed staff work* the final test is this:

> If you were the chief, would you be willing to sign the paper you have prepared, and stake your professional reputation on its being right?

If the answer is in the negative, take it back and work it over, because it is not yet *completed staff work*."

Completed Industrial Work

Industrial staff work, like Army staff work, is incomplete if you have been hasty in your investigation, failed to check the information, or left the problem unsolved. In a preliminary study, you should at least point the way to an eventual solution and make a substantial contribution.

Before turning in a report or sketch or drawing, ask yourself, "Have I really completed my assignment? Am I giving the chief what he wants? If I were the boss would I be willing to sign the report and swear to its accuracy?" If the answer is "no," your next step is obvious.

Watch for the "enemies" that prevent your work from being complete in every sense of the word. The experienced supervisor takes definite steps to resist these enemies, some of which will be examined in detail.

Passing the Buck

Some jobs and responsibilities are passed from supervisor to supervisor or executive to executive like a hot potato. Seems as though most people are afraid of getting burned. Too often the philosophy is "Let George do it." Result is that the work does not receive concentrated, intelligent attention from anybody, but gets kicked around in half-baked form. It is everybody's business in general, but nobody's business in particular.

If you do not know exactly what you personally are responsible for, make it a point to find out. A more specific outline of what's expected should be obtained from your superior. If there is any doubt whatsoever about your duties and responsibilities, request a written outline.

Avoidance of responsibility, or buck passing, is a neglect of one of the foremost duties of a supervisor. Responsibility for a complete job is yours. Just as you are held accountable for the entire job, you should in turn hold your team accountable for the portions assigned to them. Insist that they, too, perform completed staff work and restrain your temptation to do their work for them, except in cases when new employees are being oriented and trained.

PASSING THE BUCK

Your team members are responsible to you, *but they are not responsible to your boss.* When an error is made by someone in your group, you have no excuse if it is not eliminated before it leaves your hands.

Hazy Understanding of Job

As a supervisor, you realize your position as key man between the management which makes plans, decisions, policies and the men who carry out the orders. Every time an order is transmitted from the boss to you or from you to someone else, something is lost, just as, in making a record of the human voice, certain qualities are not preserved. Hence, it is doubly important that you know beyond a shadow of a doubt what the boss wants. How can you assign a job if you do not understand what it involves?

Ask any questions that are necessary when you receive your assignment. The clearer the picture you get at this time, the less you need to trouble the chief during the course of your work. This does not mean that you should contact the boss only during assignment and delivery. Naturally, he will want to keep informed about the progress of your job. However, the time to use his broader knowledge and experience is in outlining the work and in solving its tougher phases—those phases which you, because you are at the pinnacle of your potentialities, cannot solve. Like an Army chief, your boss needs answers, not questions.

HAZY UNDERSTANDING

Procrastination

Much griping is done about schedules, but they're usually not as tough as they appear. People make them tough by letting jobs go until the last few days, then working and complaining in a desperate effort to do good work in less time than should be allowed. "Do it now" is the motto to follow. As soon as an assignment is made, set your thinking processes in motion and formulate a plan of action. You need the last 10 per cent of the time allotted (or more, or less, depending on the work) to do your final checking and revising. If the job is complicated or disagreeable, there is a greater temptation to let it drift, hence more reason for losing no time in getting started, more reason for hammering at it until it's done.

Making Haste in a Hurry

There's a lot of satisfaction in completing your work a day or so early and beating a schedule. Schedules are important—they must be met *with completed staff work*. It is not wise to rush a job to the boss just to make an impression or to get it off your hands with a private reservation that after you've "made your dead line" you'll get the job back and complete it. Schedule production so you will have time to be sure you are right, and it will then be unnecessary to have neglected portions of the work reassigned, with attendant loss of time and necessity for prolonged conferences. It's embarrassing to have to retrieve a report for last-minute corrections that suddenly flash into your mind; and it's even more embarrassing to have the boss note the correction. But far worse, and inexcusable, is the situation where

THE BOSS'S BOSS DISCOVERS THE ERROR

the boss's boss has to discover the error. Minutes spent by you on thorough review to ensure completeness and accuracy can save hours for those next in line.

Other Enemies

Many other factors will interfere with successful completion of an assignment.

There is sometimes a tendency to underrate the importance of a job, either because "reasons why" are not understood by assignor or assignee or because it seems drab and routine. However, if it's worth doing, it's worth doing right.

You may have no control over last-minute changes in plans by your boss, but you can make certain that you are not guilty of the same conduct. Last-minute changes are often needed, of course, but usually because someone jumped to conclusions in the early stages of planning.

"Impossible" schedules may keep a piece of work from being

completed in the right manner. However, don't call a schedule impossible until you have exploited every possibility for saving time. Industry needs supervisors who can do the impossible.

Although a large number of concurrent projects is desirable, they should be tackled individually. Concentrate on one task at a time, lest all be incomplete.

GET ALL THE FACTS

Making thorough investigations, getting all the facts, is a characteristic associated with the experienced businessman. The enemy of completeness known as "lack of facts" should not bother him. Sometimes, however, he is inclined to forget logical methods when he delves into such matters as personnel relations or report writing. *Getting the facts* is necessary in solving any problem, technical or personnel.

20

Quiz for Supervisors

How well do you know the principles of good supervision? Only by continually improving yourself in leadership can you be effective in securing the cooperation so necessary in doing a good supervisory job.

Check yourself by means of the following quiz. Some of the statements given are true; others are false. They have purposely been made tricky in order to stimulate thought and discussion.

Place a check mark in either the True (T) or False (F) block, whichever applies. The answers considered correct by industrial-relations experts are given on pages 165 to 170. Don't look at the answers until you have finished the quiz.

The New Employee

1. If a new employee is introduced to his job in the right way during the first day or two, the supervisor's job of orientation is accomplished. T ☐ F ☐
2. The new employee should be given a specific promise as to exactly when he will get a raise and how much. T ☐ F ☐
3. The best first assignment is to have the new employee read the company's standard procedures, specifications, reports, and similar material. T ☐ F ☐
4. The first assignments of a new employee should be for practice only. T ☐ F ☐

Morale and Teamwork

5. High wages are far ahead of any other factor as a builder of good morale. T ☐ F ☐
6. No good supervisor will block the transfer of one of his employees if it means advancement for that employee. T ☐ F ☐
7. To build morale, a supervisor should treat every employee in exactly the same way in giving orders, assigning work, and administering discipline. T ☐ F ☐

TREAT EACH EMPLOYEE IN THE SAME MANNER?

8. An employee cannot be expected to be highly enthusiastic unless he understands the assignments given him and has been told something of their purpose. T ☐ F ☐

9. Criticism of an employee should be made in front of the group so they will realize they cannot get by with inferior work or infraction of rules. T ☐ F ☐

10. The assignment of difficult jobs that offer a challenge is more conducive to good morale than the assignment of easy jobs. T ☐ F ☐

11. A supervisor should not waste time by listening to suggestions from employees not directly concerned with the problem being considered. T ☐ F ☐

12. In discussing his group with his own superior, the supervisor should single out deserving members of the group for praise. T ☐ F ☐

13. Since so much of the business of an industrial company must of necessity be conducted behind closed doors, employees cannot reasonably expect to know about changes that affect them before the changes are put into practice. T ☐ F ☐

Training Employees

14. Proper training by the supervisor on the job cannot be accomplished until an analysis has been made of what the employee already knows and can do. T ☐ F ☐

15. The best training results come from a plan which hits all phases of an employee's work in a general manner. T ☐ F ☐

16. The four steps in good job instruction are *a.* prepare the worker; *b.* present the operation; *c.* stress key points; *d.* try out performance. T ☐ F ☐

Handling Grievances

17. Griping is always destructive to morale. T ☐ F ☐

18. There is no such thing as an imaginary grievance to the person possessing it. T ☐ F ☐

19. If a worker expresses a grievance to his supervisor in a long-winded, angry manner, the supervisor should get him back on the beam by disposing of the case immediately. T ☐ F ☐

THERE IS NO SUCH THING AS AN IMAGINARY GRIEVANCE?

20. If a complaining worker is wrong in his demands, the supervisor should make it easy for him to "save face" in backing down. T ☐ F ☐

Maintaining Discipline

21. Discharges of employees are more often caused by lack of social understanding (insubordination, unreliability, absenteeism, laziness, etc.) than lack of skill or technical knowledge. T ☐ F ☐

22. Inconsistent use of disciplinary measures lowers employee morale. T ☐ F ☐

23. The basic principle of discipline is to punish those who commit offenses. T ☐ F ☐

24. When an employee has committed an offense against rules and regulations, it should be called to his attention as soon as possible. T ☐ F ☐

25. After reprimanding an employee for a violation of rules or for bad conduct, the wise supervisor prevents a recurrence by occasionally reminding him of it. T ☐ F ☐

Planning

26. In planning your work, you should anticipate the unexpected so you can take care of it when it arrives. T ☐ F ☐

27. Easy jobs should always be tackled first so as to get them out of the way. T ☐ F ☐

EASY JOBS FIRST?

28. Planning a job is largely a matter of doing the job. T ☐ F ☐

29. If a supervisor can do a certain job better than anyone else in the group, he should not assign it to a subordinate. T ☐ F ☐

Giving Orders

30. A request usually gets more cooperation than any other type of order. T ☐ F ☐

31. Detailed orders are always desirable in making job assignments. T ☐ F ☐

Maintaining Quality

32. The *final responsibility* for the excellence of a job cannot be delegated to a member of a supervisor's group. T ☐ F ☐

33. An employee should not waste time reviewing his own work if it is to be checked later by another worker. T ☐ F ☐

34. The supervisor who wants high quality should point out both the good parts of a job and the errors. T ☐ F ☐

35. Whenever possible, an error should be corrected by the man who made the error. T ☐ F ☐

36. The first job done by a new employee and the first job of an unfamiliar type done by an old employee usually require more thorough checking than later assignments. T ☐ F ☐

You and the Boss

37. If you find it impossible to be loyal to your boss, it is better for you to sever connections with him. T ☐ F ☐

38. When you make a mistake, you should give careful consideration to an airtight defense for presentation to the boss. T ☐ F ☐

39. The man who has risen to an executive role is a distinct type of person with likes, dislikes, and prejudices which differ from those of the ordinary employees. T ☐ F ☐

40. The supervisor who is responsible to several bosses is in an advantageous position since he has the benefit of intimate contacts with more people in higher positions. T ☐ F ☐

Good Business Manners

41. The same general principles of supervision that apply to men are also applicable to women. T ☐ F ☐

42. Interruption of a business discussion in order to start a discussion on another subject is usually acceptable if the "interrupter" is in a higher position than that of all participants in the previous discussion. T ☐ F ☐

43. Courtesy should be shown to all associates, including bores and crackpots. T ☐ F ☐

Conferences

44. In calling a conference, it is wise to leave out people whose opinions differ widely from those of the majority. T ☐ F ☐

45. In a conference called to settle a problem, the leader's remarks should take up about one-half of the total allotted time. T ☐ F ☐

46. The best way to encourage a conference group to participate in discussion is to ask opinions of individual members. T ☐ F ☐

47. Controversial issues should always be kept in the background in a conference so that things will proceed smoothly. T ☐ F ☐

Writing Memos and Reports

48. A brief digest of your major points should usually be included in the introduction of a memorandum. T ☐ F ☐

49. If past actions related to the subject of a report have been criticized, you should include a complete defense of such actions in the report. T ☐ F ☐

50. Instructions and memos should be brief, even if this means they are not quite complete. T ☐ F ☐

DISCUSSION

1. *False.* Although proper treatment of a new employee during his first day or two is highly important, orientation is a process that should continue over a period of weeks or months. The new employee cannot possibly learn and remember all he needs to know about his job, his group, and his company in a few days.

2. *False.* Since wage raises of an employee depend on the kind of work he does, it is unwise to make a specific promise. Instead, the employee should be told generally what he can expect if he makes average progress. However, you should tell him what steps of promotion are open to him and what knowledge and training are required for each job.

3. *False.* Such information is usually quite dull and can best be studied as each new problem arises. However, the new employee should be familiar with the purpose of company manuals and know how to use them in obtaining information.

4. *False.* Assignments for practice only are discouraging to the new employee. It is better to assign actual productive work of an elementary nature which is suited to the employee's ability.

FEELING OF DIGNITY AND RESPONSIBILITY

5. *False.* Good wages are an important factor in building morale, but are not far ahead of any other factor. Elmo Roper, conductor of Fortune's Public Opinion Poll, states that people want four things from their jobs: (1) Job security—the security that comes from full employment at reasonable wages. (2) Chance to advance. (3) "Just to be treated like people." (4) Feeling of dignity and responsibility.

6. *True.* The supervisor owes it to his company to encourage the use of employees where needed most and owes it to his team members to develop them for better jobs.

7. *False.* Employees are individuals with widely varying traits and should therefore not be treated exactly alike. For example, a mild reprimand of a sensitive employee can be as effective as a bawling out of a thick-skinned person.

8. *True.* "Know-why," says Alfred H. Sinks in *The Reader's Digest,* "is the shortest, surest path to the *know-how* that turns out products faster. . . . Workers who understand their jobs don't get bored and spend their time griping; they don't quit or stay away from work except for the most urgent reasons."

9. *False.* It is a supervision axiom that criticism be made in private and praise in public. Your aim in criticism should be to obtain improvement, not to embarrass an employee.

10. *True.* True job satisfaction comes when an employee is able to utilize most of his experience and training. Although skilled employees sometimes have to work on routine, boring jobs, this is not an ideal situation.

11. *False.* You waste ideas when you fail to listen to an employee with a suggestion, even though he is not directly concerned with the problem. When you listen to suggestions, you are displaying the friendly interest that builds cooperation.

12. *True.* Employees work harder when they know they will receive recognition for jobs well done. One of the best persons to tell is your boss, preferably in the worker's presence.

13. *False.* "Tell people in advance about changes that will affect them" is one of the fundamentals of good job relations. Tell them *why* if possible. Get them to accept the change. Show how it will benefit them directly or indirectly; or if it is distasteful, show the necessity for it. (Ref. JIT card, War Manpower Commission)

14. *True.* The supervisor should compare the requirements

for a job with the worker's training and experience, so that he can provide on-the-job training. Such an analysis also aids in making suitable job assignments.

15. *False.* Training should be comprehensive and concentrated on certain phases of an employee's work. Hitting the high spots gives only a superficial knowledge.

16. *False.* "Stress key points" is a part of presenting the operation, and the important follow-up step has been omitted. Your JIT card lists these four rules on "How to Instruct": (1) Prepare the worker. (2) Present the operation (stressing key points). (3) Try out performance. (4) Follow up.

PUTTING HIM ON HIS OWN

The last step means putting him on his own. Designate to whom he goes for help. Check frequently. Encourage questions. Get him to look for key points as he progresses. Taper off extra coaching and close follow-up. (Refer to JIT card, War Manpower Commission.)

17. *False.* Griping of a constructive nature calls attention to grievances on which you should take immediate corrective action. Griping is also a healthy way of letting off steam. A wise supervisor gets many a good idea by listening to gripes. However, if the grievance is not corrected, griping may also be destructive to morale.

18. *True.* To the person possessing it, an imaginary grievance is just as real as a true grievance. Imaginary grievances should be given careful attention, not passed over lightly. Demonstrate

to the employee that he has no reasonable cause for the imaginary complaint.

19. *False.* Don't jump to conclusions. Allow the employee to present his case in detail. This will give you a better basis on which to make a decision and will help make the employee feel that he is getting a fair hearing.

20. *True.* If the worker has no real cause for complaint, your aim is to persuade him of this fact. Why defeat your purpose by making it difficult for him to withdraw his complaint?

21. *True.* Dr. John M. Brewer of Harvard analyzed 4,375 cases where discharges were necessary. He found that 62.4 per cent were caused by lack of social understanding (insubordination, unreliability, absenteeism, laziness, etc.). Only 34.2 per cent were caused by lack of skill or technical knowledge.

22. *True.* If a supervisor is strict and severe one day and allows anything to get by the next, his team members will become confused and irritated.

23. *False.* The basic principle of discipline is *to prevent recurrences* of violations rather than to punish those responsible for past violations.

24. *True.* The best time to take action is after the first offense, when mild measures may prove very effective.

25. *False.* If you do keep reminding an employee of a past violation, it's a confession that you have failed to make an effective reprimand, and it may earn for you a reputation as a nagger.

26. *True.* You should be prepared to take care of unexpected problems. For example, good planning calls for training of employees to do the work of others (including yourself) in case of unexpected absences.

27. *False.* The most urgent job should usually be tackled first, no matter whether it is easy or difficult. When two jobs are of equal importance, it is often best to tackle the toughest one first to forestall the natural tendency to stall.

28. *False.* Planning means outlining or scheduling a method or scheme of action, procedure, or arrangement. It is largely a matter of advance thinking.

29. *False.* Too many supervisors have work piled up on their desks because they have not learned to shift some of their responsibilities and worries to their subordinates.

30. *True.* The request is the friendly way of issuing in-

structions. It puts people at ease, prevents irritations, builds cooperation.

31. *False.* Implied or suggestive orders are most desirable for experienced and dependable employees. Use detailed orders for new, undependable, or inexperienced employees and in case of complicated, infrequent, or special assignments.

32. *True.* Although responsibilities should be wisely delegated to members of your group, you as the supervisor are *finally* responsible for both quality and speed.

33. *False.* High-quality work results only when the person doing the work is sufficiently interested to review his own work and correct errors.

34. *True.* Constructive criticism of a job involves both pointing out errors (as a preventive action) and praising good work (for the sake of morale).

35. *True.* When a person has to correct his own errors, the necessity for doing high-quality work is emphasized and in many cases (especially with a new employee) valuable knowledge may be gained.

36. *True.* The thorough checking of a first job ensures the formation of proper habits right at the start.

37. *True.* Your own work and that of your boss and your company depend on loyalty.

38. *False.* Admit your mistakes. Defending them wastes time and irritates everyone concerned.

39. *False.* Bosses are human beings, too.

40. *False.* Although it is an advantage to have contacts with many executives, no supervisor should have to be directly responsible to more than one man at the same time.

41. *True.* Women in business resent being treated as a special class of people. But each employee, man or woman, is an individual with varying characteristics which should be considered by a supervisor.

42. *False.* Any but the most imperative interruptions are discourteous.

43. *True.* It may annoy you to have to be courteous to some people, but such courtesy is usually rewarded.

44. *False.* People with opinions differing from those of the majority may have much to contribute in a conference. The majority is often wrong in its opinions.

45. *False.* A conference leader should generally take up

no more than 15 to 20 per cent of the allotted time. His job is to encourage others to talk while he listens, to keep the conference on the beam, and to direct the discussion toward a conclusion.

46. *False.* Asking an individual member of a conference for his opinion is one of the worst (and most common) ways of attempting to stimulate a discussion. Such a request puts the member on the spot at a time when he may not be prepared to answer. If necessary to use a direct question, ask for specific information which you know he can supply. The best method for a conference leader to use, however, is to prepare his comments so that they will lead to spontaneous discussion. Occasionally, a conference leader may make deliberate misstatements in order to get a discussion started.

47. *False.* Controversial issues pertinent to the subject should be dragged out into the open for settlement. Conferences are intended to iron out differences.

48. *True.* Give your reader a brief summary at the very beginning for his convenience.

49. *False.* There is no need to make a lengthy defense of what you've done in the past. Too much time is wasted by those who feel that they must present an alibi for every doubtful action.

50. *False.* Instructions and memos should be like a bathing suit: Complete enough to cover the subject, brief enough to be interesting.

21

Books for Supervisors

Now that the hard-boiled supervisor with the manner of a gorilla is getting to be as obsolete as hoop skirts, it's not enough, today, to have "handled men" before. Fortunately, studies of practical experience and industrial psychology have brought out many scientific aspects of supervision. A wealth of useful books is available for the sergeants

GORILLA SUPERVISOR OBSOLETE

and officers of industry who want to improve their methods of securing production by means of *teamwork*.

Know People

For a supervisor to get what he wants (get things done right, quickly) he needs to know a lot about *Getting Along with People*. And that's the title of a worth-while background book by Milton Wright (Whittlesey House, McGraw-Hill Book Company,

Inc., New York, 1936). It's middle of the road—not too light and popular, yet not academic and stilted.

How to Work with People by Sumner Harwood (Cambridge Analytical Services, Cambridge, Mass., 1940) has valuable suggestions for all workers but is of prime importance to the supervisor. It deals with scientific methods of securing cooperation.

Eleven easy-to-understand rules for leadership are explained in *The Technique of Handling People*, by Donald A. Laird and Eleanor C. Laird (Whittlesey House, McGraw-Hill Book Company, Inc., New York, 1943). "If you are expecting something complicated, change your mind," says the author in giving these rules:

"1. Ask questions to win cooperation.

"2. Be brief to clear up troubles.

"3. Confident bearing to control others.

"4. Directness to reach into people's minds.

"5. Earnestness to arouse enthusiasm.

"6. Friendliness to overcome opposition.

"7. Good-finding to mobilize ability.

"8. Harness criticism in a way to win appreciation.

"9. Increase others' self-esteem to cultivate loyalty.

"10. Jingle praise to secure best efforts.

"11. Know your people to generate harmony."

Leading the Team

Packed with information of interest to all who supervise is *Personal Leadership in Industry* by David R. Craig and W. W. Charters (McGraw-Hill Book Company, Inc., New York, 1941). Typical chapter headings are Teamwork, Kindliness without Weakness, Obtaining the Best Efforts of Subordinates, Training on the Job, Improvement of Quality Standards, and Leading without Bossing.

Why it's better to lead than to boss is told in *The Art of Leadership* by Ordway Tead (Whittlesey House, McGraw-Hill Book Company, Inc., New York, 1935). He explodes the viewpoint that leaders are born and not made, and goes ahead to show how leadership qualities can be developed and supervisory skill strengthened.

The Women

It may be true that mere man can never understand women. But the supervisor who is on his toes will want to read Donald Laird's *The Psychology of Supervising the Working Woman*

(McGraw-Hill Book Company, Inc., New York, 1942). The author points out the excellent work done by women working under capable supervisors, who take into account the fundamental differences between men and women. It's a book you'll want to read from cover to cover.

For Brass Hats

Executive-type supervisors, such as department heads, encounter broader problems which are comprehensively treated in the *Elements of Supervision* by William R. Spriegel and Edward Schulz (John Wiley & Sons, Inc., New York, 1942). Much of the material in this book is based on the curriculum developed for supervisors and prospective supervisors in a large enterprise.

For All Supervisors

A manual for all leaders from the executive to the front-line supervisor is Alfred M. Cooper's *How to Supervise People* (McGraw-Hill Book Company, Inc., New York, 1941). It reports specific solutions for supervisory problems developed in conferences at which tested ideas were presented. Advice is also given to the worker who wants to get in line for a supervisory job.

For Topkicks

Modern Industrial Leadership by Jerald A. Foster Brannon (National Foremen's Institute, 1942) is a series of ten lecture-conferences covering the following subjects: Essentials of Leadership, Starting New Workers Right, Training New Workers, Giving Instructions, Maintaining Discipline, Knowing Your Worker, Establishing Confidence, Delegating Responsibility, Budgeting Time, Building Morale.

Pep on the Job

In *How to Create Job Enthusiasm*, Carl Heyel (McGraw-Hill Book Company, Inc., New York, 1942) analyzes the entire

problem of job enthusiasm. How do some leaders keep people on their toes? Techniques that are in effective use today are described in this book.

The Fundamentals

For many years the extension service of Pennsylvania State College has been training supervisors for industrial companies. Results of this experience are published in a recent series. *Do You Want to Be a Foreman?* by Albert Walton (McGraw-Hill Book Company, Inc., New York, 1941) is an orientation manual for the prospective supervisor. *The Fundamentals of Industrial Psychology* (McGraw-Hill Book Company, Inc., New York, 1941), also by Walton, is a nontechnical book stressing important psychological principles. *Industrial Supervision—Organization*, by Vernon G. Schaeffer and Willis Wissler (McGraw-Hill Book Company, Inc., New York, 1941), is a background book on industrial organization, job evaluation, training, and planning. The same authors have also written *Industrial Supervision—Controls* (McGraw-Hill Book Company, Inc., New York, 1941), which deals with the personal problems of a supervisor.

People Who Gripe

A practical workbook is *How to Handle Grievances* by Glenn Gardiner (Elliot Service Company, New York, 1937), who has been a skilled mechanic, foreman, personnel manager, and

assistant works manager. Just as fires at their start can be put out with a teacupful of water, serious personnel troubles can often be averted by proper handling of small grievances.

Other Books

The Technique of Building Personal Leadership, Donald A. Laird (Whittlesey House, McGraw-Hill Book Company, Inc., New York, 1944).

Foremanship Fundamentals, A. L. Kress (McGraw-Hill Book Company, Inc., New York, 1942).

The Managerial Revolution; What Is Happening to the World, James Burnham (The John Day Company, New York, 1941).

Middle Management; the Job of the Junior Administrator, Mrs. M. C. Niles (Harper & Brothers, New York, 1941).

Creative Management, Ordway Tead (Association Press, New York, 1935).

The Science of Work, M. S. Viteles (W. W. Norton & Company, Inc., New York, 1934).

Principles of Industrial Management for Engineers, L. P. Alford (The Ronald Press Company, New York, 1940).

Better Foremanship, G. L. Gardiner (McGraw-Hill Book Company, Inc., New York, 1941).

Effective Foremanship, H. B. Maynard, ed. (McGraw-Hill Book Company, Inc., New York, 1941).

New Techniques for Supervisors and Foremen, Albert Walton (McGraw-Hill Book Company, Inc., New York, 1940).

The Psychology of Dealing with People, Wendell White (The Macmillan Company, New York, 1936).

How to Use Psychology in Business, D. A. Laird (McGraw-Hill Book Company, Inc., New York, 1942).

Getting Things Done in Business, E. B. Wilson (McGraw-Hill Book Company, Inc., New York, 1942).

Management and Morale, F. J. Roethlisberger (Harvard University Press, Cambridge, Mass., 1941).

Human-Relations Manual for Executives, Carl Heyel (McGraw-Hill Book Company, Inc., New York, 1939).

The Technique of Executive Control, E. H. Schell (McGraw-Hill Book Company, Inc., New York, 1934).

Top-management Organization and Control, P. E. Holden and others (Stanford University Press, Stanford University, California, 1941).

Appendix

An Employee Opinion Poll

Authors' Note: Although the technique of conducting employee opinion surveys is a problem for the industrial-relations staff, supervisors should be acquainted with the type of information that can be obtained. Many so-called "morale" surveys have been conducted using questionnaires received only from employees interested enough to answer a long list of questions and without regard for securing a true cross section of opinion. The following is a report on an employee survey, made in 1944, which attempted to apply methods used by advertising and public-opinion researchers to the industrial-relations field.

How effectively engineering supervisors at The Glenn L. Martin Company had outlined their employees' duties and responsibilities, gradually increased their responsibilities, given needed assistance, and delegated detail work, was determined by a Gallup-like survey of a scientifically selected cross section comprising 10 per cent of employees, whether project engineer or clerk, design engineer or typist. The survey included five questions, all related to the subject Responsibility. Those interviewed to secure opinions were picked by I.B.M. machine to eliminate prejudice. I.B.M. cards were arranged by major supervisory groups and job titles to obtain 10 per cent in each of these classes. By substituting a few cards, picked at random, it was possible to balance the selected sample and have the proper proportion of men and women, supervisors and non-supervisors, etc.

The purpose of the survey was to obtain information on the effectiveness of supervisors along several lines, as shown by one yardstick—employee opinion. Survey conductors, who thought that outlining and delegating responsibilities might show up as a general problem throughout the department, were pleased to find this was not the case.

Favorable replies were given on all five questions by the majority of those interviewed. Unfavorable replies were remarkably few in number. Other findings of the survey:

1. There is a distinct advantage in having supervisors explain duties and responsibilities to their employees, rather than have employees find out for themselves.
2. More supervisors than nonsupervisors believed their superiors handled detail work that should be delegated.
3. More women than men stated that their responsibilities had been "increased gradually" in 1943, but the differences in opinion between men and women were not great on any of the questions.
4. There were no startling differences in opinion between college graduates and nongraduates and between technical and nontechnical employees.

It is generally accepted that a supervisor should clearly explain each employee's duties and responsibilities. The results

EXPLAIN DUTIES AND RESPONSIBILITIES

of the survey showed that when this was done there was a 3 to 1 better chance that the employee was "unquestionably clear" than when he found out for himself.

How clear	*How explained*		
	"Found out for myself," per cent	*"Supervisor partly explained," per cent*	*"Supervisor explained," per cent*
Vague idea	4	0	0
Fairly clear	18	7	4
Generally clear	61	64	45
Unquestionably clear	17	29	51
Total	100	100	100

The above results were obtained by comparing answers to Questions 1 and 2 in the survey. These results, given below, show that about 90 per cent are either "generally clear" or "unquestionably clear" on duties and responsibilities, but that 27 per cent stated they "found out for myself." Only 17 per cent of this latter group state they are "unquestionably clear" as

DO YOU HAVE A CLEAR IDEA?

to their duties and responsibilities. Questions 1 and 2 were the following:

Do you have a clear idea of your duties and responsibilities—that is, what's expected of you in your job?

	Per Cent
Vague idea	1.5
Fairly clear	8.0
Generally clear	50.5
Unquestionably clear	40.0

Has your supervisor ever outlined your duties and responsibilities?

	Per Cent
Supervisor explained	65.5
Found out for myself	27.0
Still in dark	0.5
Partly "Supervisor explained" and partly "Found out for myself"[1]	7.0

The above results compare favorably with a previous survey made in February, 1943, when employees were asked, "Has your supervisor made clear to you your duties and responsibilities?" The answers were: 14 per cent "vaguely"; 38 per cent "fairly clear"; 48 per cent "completely clear." By contrast, only 1.5 per cent now state they have only a "vague idea" as to duties and responsibilities.

Most engineering employees state they have been given increased responsibilities, but more women than men report "gradual increase in responsibility," as shown by answers to Question 3:

Since the first of the year, have you been made responsible for more work or for higher types of work than in 1943?

	Men, per cent	Women, per cent	Total, per cent
Gradual increase in responsibility	54	76	63
Abrupt increase in responsibility	17	3	10.5
Less responsibility	3	3	3.5
No change	26	18	23
Total	100	100	100

[1] This situation was not included on the survey sheet but was written in by 7 per cent of those interviewed.

GIVING ASSISTANCE

There were very few complaints about not enough or too much assistance by the supervisor, employees reported in answer to Question 4:

When you are given a job to do, does your superior give you all the assistance you need?

	Per Cent
All I need	90.5
Not enough	8
Too much	1.5
Total	100

Only 21 per cent of nonsupervisors interviewed stated that their superiors handled detail work that should have been delegated, but 37 per cent of the supervisors held this opinion.

On jobs assigned to you, do your superiors handle any detail work that should be handled by you or others in your group?

	Nonsupervisors, per cent	*Supervisors, per cent*	*Total, per cent*
Hardly any	76	63	73
Some	21	37	24.5
A great deal	3	0	2.5

Index